David M. Schleser

Piranh

Everything about Selection, Care, Nutrition,
Diseases, Breeding, and Behavior

With 64 Color Photographs

Illustrations by David Wenzel

BARRON'S

Dedication

Dedicated to my parents for their great tolerance, understanding, patience, and constant support.

All inquiries should be addressed to:
Barron's Educational Series, Inc.
250 Wireless Boulevard
Hauppauge, NY 11788

International Standard Book No. 0-8120-9916-8

Library of Congress Catalog Card No. 96-37938

Library of Congress Cataloging-in-Publication Data
Schleser, David M.
    Piranhas : everything about origins, care, feeding, diseases, breeding, and behavior / David M. Schleser ; illustrations by David Wenzel.
        p.   cm.
    Includes bibliographical references (p.   ) and index.
        ISBN 0-8120-9916-8
        1. Piranhas. I. Title.
SF458.P57S36   1997
639.3′748—dc21
96-37938
CIP

Printed in Hong Kong

987654321

About the Author

David M. Schleser was trained as a dentist, a profession which he practiced for 19 years. In 1982 he changed careers to aquatic biology, and later served for over five years as the Curator/Aquatic Biologist for the Dallas Aquarium, Dallas, Texas. He recently resigned this position to work full time for Nature's Images, Inc., a natural history photography and writing company which he helped establish. Since 1988, he has traveled regularly to the rain forests of Costa Rica, and the Amazon regions of Peru and Brazil, for purposes of research and photography. He frequently serves as the tour leader for Amazon River ecological and tropical fish study expeditions. David Schleser's photographs and writings have appeared in many scientific and popular publications. He is also a Tetra speaker and presents many lectures on aquatic subjects to aquarium societies throughout the United States and Canada. His major ichthyological interests are South American characins, the Centrarchids of North America and desert fishes.

Photo Credits

Jeff Cardwell: page 79 bottom; Dr. Devon Graham: page 84; Zig Leszczynski: inside front cover, inside back cover, page 74; Dr. Leo Nico: pages 25 top, 78 bottom, 82; Dr. Kirk O. Winemiller: pages 14 right, 16, 24 bottom, 75 top right and bottom, 78 top, 80 top, 81 top and bottom; all other photos provided by the author.

Important Note

Anyone keeping piranhas as pets must use extreme caution at all times when handling them or servicing the piranha aquarium. The razor-sharp teeth and powerful jaws of large piranhas are able to inflict severe flesh wounds, and are even capable of cleanly amputating a finger. For this reason, hobbyists with small children are strongly advised not to keep piranhas as pets. A doctor should immediately be seen for the treatment of any bite from a piranha.

When electrical appliances are used in the presence of water, there is always the potential for life-threatening accidents. Be certain to read Electrical Safety Concerns on page 35.

Contents

Preface

This book is an attempt to enlighten the reader about what is now known about piranhas, dispel a few widely held beliefs, raise some as yet unanswered questions, and provide the hobbyist with information needed to successfully maintain and possibly reproduce these charismatic fishes in their aquariums. An important section at the back of the book is devoted to photographs and data of a cross-section of piranha species, a few of which have only recently been described.

With so little known about piranha biology and behavior, aquarists have the unique opportunity to provide significant contributions to our knowledge of piranhas and help fill many of the voids in our understanding of these uniquely adapted fishes.

A word about the photographs: With few exceptions, the photographs of piranhas used in this book were taken in the field immediately after capture, and are not of aquarium specimens. These images are less esthetically pleasing than those taken in well-aquascaped aquariums, but they are the best means of conveying to the reader the true colors of piranhas in nature. Wherever possible, locale data is provided.

Acknowledgments

The author would like to recognize the following people for their indispensable help in the preparation of this book: Leo Nico permitted me access to his (unpublished) Doctoral dissertation on piranha ecology, provided important photographs of some lesser known piranha species, and reviewed the first draft of the manuscript for errors in taxonomy and natural biology; Kirk O. Winemiller provided many papers he and others authored concerning piranha biology and natural history, and graciously supplied me with some excellent photographs used in this book; William Fink supplied reprints of his papers concerning piranha taxonomy and helped in the identification of specimens collected during my South American travels; Stanley Weitzman was, as always, a tremendous help in discussing questions involving characoid taxonomy. A special thanks to: Michael La Fuente and Adrienne Thacker for helping in the translation of Spanish- and French-language publications, respectively, into English; Paul V. Loiselle for his continual help and advice; and Roger Klocek for information concerning captive reproduction of various piranha species at the Shedd Aquarium. David T. and Deborah L. Roberts proofread the first draft of the manuscript and provided many important suggestions. Last, but not least, I cannot thank enough the many people I met in my visits to the Amazon region who, though too numerous to individually name, were indispensable in the obtaining of needed specimens and providing me with firsthand knowledge concerning piranhas.

Understanding Piranhas

Worldwide, the word "piranha" elicits greater name recognition than almost any other group of fishes. It might therefore come as a surprise that most of the commonly held beliefs concerning these species are either incomplete, oversimplified, or grossly inaccurate. Statements such as that of the eminent icthyologist, Dr. George Myers, that "the piranha is the most dangerous fish in the Amazon and perhaps in the world" often result in the erroneous impression that either there is only one species of piranha or that they all have the same habits.

Within recent years, both field and laboratory research involving the biology of piranhas have greatly expanded our limited knowledge about these fishes. Much of what we are learning about their behavior, senses, taxonomy, and developmental biology is unexpected and often nothing short of astounding. Piranhas are turning out to be a behaviorally complex and very successful group of fishes of which we must change some of our most widely held beliefs.

Much remains to be learned about piranhas. The exact number of species has yet to be determined and we are only beginning to understand their biology, behavior, and impact upon the other species that share their environment.

One thing that has not changed is our fascination with piranhas and their popularity as aquarium fish. This will surely increase as lesser-known species become more available.

Origin of the Name Piranha

The word "piranha," of Tupi-Guarani Indian derivation, has long been used throughout a large portion of the Amazon basin. In the Tupi language *pira* means fish, whereas *ranha* (or *sanha*) refers to teeth. The piranha is therefore appropriately known as the toothed fish. The correct pronunciation of the word piranha is pee-ron-yah, with the accent on the second syllable, and not the commonly heard pir-ann-uh.

It has been written that the word piranha means scissors. The fallacy in this argument becomes obvious when

Throughout the piranhas' range, the native peoples show little concern for their cosmopolitan presence. Photographed in the Peruvian Amazon along the Marañon River.

Seining for piranhas and other fishes in a drying floodplain lake.

piranha. In many parts of the Amazon only the flesh-eating species are called piranhas, the harmless forms being known as *chupita* or *pirambeba.* In the Llanos region of Venezuela piranhas are called *caribe* (cah-ree-bay) after the once fearsome Carib Indians. This is reflected in the Latin name of one of the larger and more aggressive Venezuelan species, *Pygocentrus cariba.*

Evolution of the Myth

Most of us have heard the horrific stories: people in boats having fingers amputated by piranhas after absent-mindedly trailing them in the water; ranchers who routinely sacrifice a cow to appease the piranhas' savage hunger before driving their cattle across a river or stream; the foolish bather being reduced to a skeleton in a matter of minutes by a hoard of "bloodthirsty" piranhas. In fact, probably we have all seen at least one sensationalized horror film casting the piranha as the villain.

Early Accounts

Among the earliest accounts of piranhas to reach Europe were those in George Margraves' *Historia Naturalis Brasiliae,* published in Amsterdam in 1648. All the elements of horror so common in later tales are included in this work. He emphasized their sharp teeth and savage nature, the danger of entering piranha-infested waters, and their ability to cleanly bite off chunks of flesh. In the 1790s the explorer and naturalist Alexander Von Humboldt's folio volumes documenting his South American travels devote two pages to piranhas, stressing their vicious nature. He refers to them as one of South America's greatest scourges. In his personal narrative about life on the Orinoco, which was published between 1816 and 1831, he wrote:

". . . our Indians caught with a hook the fish known in the country by the

we realize that these fishes were called by the name piranha long before the Europeans introduced scissors to South America. The truth is exactly the opposite: It has long been the custom for Amazonian natives to use a dried piranha jaw, with the razor-sharp teeth still attached, as a tool that is a cross between a knife and a pair of scissors. It is no wonder that when these Indians were shown their first scissors, they called them piranhas. To this day, in certain areas of the Brazilian Amazon, scissors are still known by this name.

Amazonian people recognize differences between the various species of piranhas. Often this is not based upon taxonomic principles but upon differences in body shape, color, and potential danger to humans. Thus, *Serrasalmus rhombeus* is known as *piranha preta* (black piranha) or *piranha blanco* (white piranha), depending upon the age of the fish; the widespread red-bellied piranha, *Pygocentrus nattereri,* is called *piranha vermillia* in Brazil and *piranha roja* in Peru, both meaning red piranha. *S. elongatus,* because of its long pointed head, is sometimes known as the *piranha mucura*—the opossum name of *caribe* or *caribito* [Caribe in the Spanish language signifies cannibal] . because no other fish has such a thirst for blood. It attacks bathers and swimmers, from whom it bites away considerable pieces of flesh. The Indians dread extremely these caribes. . . ."

Later Accounts

Most of what Americans first learned about piranhas came from the writings of no less an eminent person than the explorer, big game hunter, soldier, and twenty-sixth president of the United States, Theodore Roosevelt. In his book *Through the Brazilian Wilderness,* published in 1914, he recounted sensationalized tales of the piranhas' ferocity. Included is a story of a rider who, after falling from his horse while fording a stream, was attacked by a school of voracious piranhas and quickly reduced to a skeleton.

There is even disagreement about the ferocity of piranhas in the writings of more modern authors. Brazilian anthropologist Harold Schultz, after spending more than two decades traveling widely throughout Brazil, flatly states: "In all these years I have never had a harmful experience with these greatly feared piranhas." He then strongly admonishes writers of books that include what he refers to as "absurd stories" (about piranhas) and is particularly offended when they are purported to be serious scientific notes. He does admit to knowing people who have received piranha bites, but stresses that they were all minor and none were life-threatening.

The ichthyologist Dr. George S. Myers was a bit more cautious. He stated in *The Piranha Book* (see Useful Literature, page 85), that four species "are always dangerous to man" and then describes the piranhas that we now include in the genus *Pygocentrus.* Referring to this group, he wrote that a piranha has ". . . teeth so sharp and jaws so strong that it can chop out a

The larger piranha species, such as these two black piranhas, Serrasalmus rhombeus, *are a common item in the local cuisine.*

piece of flesh from a man or alligator as neatly as a razor, or clip off a finger or toe, bone and all, with the dispatch of a meat cleaver." There is little doubt that piranhas are capable of such mutilation. The question that still remains is how often they perform it!

Seeking the Truth About Piranhas

Any traveler to the areas of South America inhabited by piranhas will routinely observe children playing and swimming unconcerned—and unharmed—in the rivers. Men are often seen in water over their heads setting gill nets or pulling large seines while the women are washing clothes in the shallows. What are we to believe? Are these people ignoring a real danger or is the malevolent reputation of piranhas the product of overactive imaginations?

In my many trips to the Peruvian and Brazilian Amazon doing research or leading tropical fish study expeditions there has not been a single incident where a member of our party has been molested by piranhas. I feel this is significant because we always spend much of our time in the water pulling nets, setting fish traps (some with bait), and swimming across or fording streams and small rivers. We often catch large numbers of the supposedly highly dangerous red-bellied piranha, *Pygocentrus nattereri.* At times one of our group will be catching piranhas on a hook and line while others of us are bathing or swimming nearby. I have often asked Amazonian natives whether they fear piranhas. More often than not they smile and say that the most dangerous piranha is a live one flopping in the bottom of a dugout canoe. They often dramatize their story by curling a toe under their foot to simulate a piranha amputation.

Weighing the Evidence

Does this mean that piranhas should be considered harmless? I wouldn't go that far. All the stories about piranha ferocity cannot be ignored and some are undoubtedly true. We must first realize that only a small percentage of piranha species have the potential to be of danger to humans, and even these require special conditions to elicit such aggressive behavior. The sharpness and strength of their teeth and jaws is a frightening reality. It appears that how they act is highly dependent upon sets of conditions and other stimuli we do not as yet fully understand. One often reads that when *Pygocentrus* species are trapped in isolated drying lakes where they have exhausted their food supply, they are a potential danger to any animal entering the water. Yet I have routinely collected piranhas with the use of seine nets in just such areas without incident. Probably the risk of injury is much greater in murky waters contaminated by blood and offal and I

would definitely avoid entering such areas. It goes without saying that captured piranhas of all types should be handled with extreme care. Attempts to document supposedly fatal attacks by piranhas on humans have more often than not determined that the person had first drowned and the body was then scavenged by piranhas and other fishes.

In some parts of South America, piranhas are notorious for attacking the genitals and udders of wading cattle. This behavior is responsible for *P. cariba* being known locally in Venezuela as the *capaburro,* or donkey castrator. The herpetologist William Lamar recounted a story to me of particularly aggressive *P. cariba* in the Venezuelan Llanos. These piranhas inhabited the waters below a waterbird rookery and appeared to subsist mainly upon fledglings and other food items that fell from the nests. They were so conditioned to this food source that anything that hit the surface of the water or caused a splash was instantly attacked. Not the ideal swimming hole!

One fact that cannot be refuted is that there are many more piranhas eaten by humans than there are humans eaten by piranhas! Throughout the piranhas' range they are popular food fish and are served in a variety of ways. The simplest way is to boil them with rice, beans, and spices to make a soup or stew. Another common method of preparation is to first make numerous closely spaced parallel incisions through the skin, rubbing in some spices, and then broil or roast them over an open fire. I have eaten many piranhas and found the flesh to be flaky and tender, but not particularly tasty and full of numerous fine bones.

Introducing the Piranha

Classification

Piranhas and their relatives are classified as characoid fishes. Although there has been some disagreement among authorities concerning piranha taxonomy, it is now generally accepted that they belong to the subfamily Serrasalminae, a division of the large and diverse characin family. In addition to the piranhas, this subfamily also includes the various pacus and silver dollars of the genera *Colossoma, Piaractus, Mylossoma, Myleus, Metynnis,* etc.

Some of the anatomic characteristics of the characoids are the presence of scales, teeth, and an adipose fin, but some rare or unique species may lack one of the above structures. There is never a spiny region of the dorsal and anal fins as seen in more advanced fishes such as cichlids. Characins are among the fishes that possess a series of modified bones or ossicles that connects the swim bladder with the internal ear that greatly enhances their hearing. This structure is called the Weberian apparatus.

Fishes of the subfamily Serrasalminae are recognized by the presence of a unique combination of characteristics not found in other characins. The name Serrasalminae, meaning salmon with a saw, refers to the saw-toothed ventral keel found in all fishes within this taxonomic unit. This keel is made up of a row of modified pointed scales called serrae, which vary in number among the different species. Serrasalmines also have numerous small scales and are rather deep bodied, laterally compressed, and slab-sided; some are almost disk-shaped. A peculiarity seen in adult specimens of many piranha species is a slightly asymmetric tail, the lower lobe being a bit larger than the upper. The reason for this anatomic modification is not known.

Teeth and Jaws

Another important taxonomic feature of piranhas is their unique dentition. The teeth and immensely powerful jaws of the true piranhas are adapted for cleanly biting off pieces of food, which we will see is not always of an animal nature. There is a single row of triangular, razor-sharp, interlocking teeth in each jaw. When the mouth is closed, the points of the upper teeth fit into the notches of the lower row. On each tooth there is a cusp or point that fits tightly inside a recess of the adjacent tooth, effectively securing together

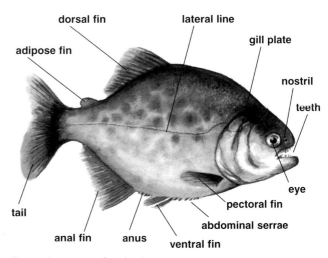

External anatomy of a piranha.

This silver dollar, Metznnis *sp., above, and red-bellied pacu,* Piaractus brachypomus (bidens), *below, belong to the subfamily Serrasalminae.*

all the teeth in each half of a jaw into a single functional element. Each row of teeth is so intimately locked together that, instead of shedding and replacing worn teeth one at a time, an entire row on one side is lost and replaced as a unit. Only one side is shed at a time, permitting piranhas to continue feeding while renewing their dentition. The teeth of piranha relatives, such as the

Double row of teeth typical of the pacus. This is Piaractus brachypomus *(syn.* bidens*), the red-bellied pacu. Rio Orosa, Peru.*

pacus, are noninterlocking and arranged in double rows.

Genera of Piranhas

The fish we commonly refer to as piranhas are now considered to include five separate genera. These are *Pygopristis, Pristobrycon, Serrasalmus, Pygocentrus,* and *Catoprion.* Each is distinguished by differences in tooth structure and skeletal anatomy. These differences are reflected in their diets and behavioral biology. All except *Catoprion* were formerly combined in the single genus *Serrasalmus.* It is unfortunate that the common name of *Catoprion mento*— the wimple piranha—incorporates the word piranha. Although belonging to the subfamily Serrasalminae, it is only distantly related to all the other species known as piranhas and it lacks the interlocking saw-like single row of teeth in both jaws that are unique to the true piranhas.

The exact number of piranha species has not yet been determined, but it is estimated that there are at least 20. Some have not yet been scientifically described, while others have been described more than once under

This red-throated piranha, Serrasalmus spilopleura, *displays the single row of triangular teeth characteristic of the piranhas. Rio Orosa, Peru.*

a variety of names. Many piranhas undergo major changes in shape as they mature, and within a species there is variation in coloration and pattern related to age, size, sexual state, and environmental factors. The accurate ranges of many have not yet been fully determined. It will take some time until all this is sorted out.

Pygopristis is a monotypic (containing only one species) genus with *P. denticulatus* being the single recognized species. It is the most primitive of the piranhas and the least adapted to a predatory existence. The musculature and anatomy of its jaws are relatively weak, and its teeth have five

An unidentified piranha of the genus Serrasalmus, *collected near the Town of Yanashi on the Peruvian Amazon.*

The five-cusped piranha, Pygopristis denticulatus, *is the only known species within this genus. Collected off the Rio Dimini, a tributary of the Rio Negro, Brazil.*

A young specimen of a Pristobrycon *piranha, probably P. serrulatus. Rio Nanay, Peru.*

This Serrasalmus *piranha (possibly S. spilopleura) clearly demonstrates the concave outline to the nape region.*

cusps, giving them a serrated appearance. The specific epithet *denticulatus* means "with small cusps or serrations" and refers to this dental anatomy. The bilobed anal fin of adult males is reminiscent of the silver dollars of the genus *Myleus.* It appears to be widely distributed within the Amazon Basin, Orinoco, and Guiana drainages.

The *Pristobrycon* piranhas more closely resemble our mental picture of what a piranha should look like, but tend to be deeper in body and more disk-like in shape. Their jaws are relatively small, and in addition to the jaw teeth there are a few blunt teeth present on the inner roof of the mouth. These are the piranhas often referred to as *pirambebas* in the literature.

The remaining two genera, *Serrasalmus* and *Pygocentrus,* comprise the typical piranhas. *Serrasalmus* species have powerful jaws with large teeth and an additional eight to ten

Piranhas of the genus Pygocentrus *have a convexly rounded profile to the head and nape region. This is a red-bellied piranha, P. natereri.*

Juvenile black piranha, S. rhombeus *(above), and red-bellied piranha, P. nattereri (below). These fish are less than one inch in length.*

well-developed, pointed teeth on the palate. The dorsal contour of their "neck" region tends to be concave in outline and their bodies diamond-shaped in profile. Some *Serrasalmus* piranhas reach a very large size. In the Xingu river of Brazil *S. manueli* is known to reach a length of almost two feet (61 cm) and a weight of five pounds (2.27 kg). There have been reports of Peruvian *S. rhombeus* that were considerably heavier. Contrary to their often fearsome appearance and intimidating appearance, no piranha of this genus has ever been documented to be a threat to man.

The three reputedly dangerous piranhas are all included within the genus *Pygocentrus.* The generic names *Taddyella* and *Rooseveltiella,* both honoring Theodore "Teddy" Roosevelt, have been previously applied to members of this genus (*Taddyella* is based on a misspelling of Roosevelt's nickname Teddy) and still can be found in the literature. *Pygocentrus* species characteristically have a convex dorsal profile to the region of the back and head anterior to the dorsal fin, and a very heavy and strong lower jaw. They have wider and more powerfully muscled heads and jaws than any other group of piranhas, and their palate is never toothed. Living specimens of all three species show much orange-red color to the breast and abdomen and are all often referred to as red-bellied piranhas. To avoid confusion, I will reserve this title for *P. nattereri.* This Amazonian species has the widest range, and is the most commonly imported and best-known piranha in thc hobby. *P. piraya,* from the Rio Sao Francisco of Southeastern Brazil is the largest, reaching a size of at least 20 inches (51 cm). It is said to be greatly feared by the natives of this region, although information to the contrary is just as often heard. *P. cariba* (formerly *P. notatus*) from the Orinoco river drainage is easily identified by the large black spot on its side behind the head. Often called the Orinoco red-bellied piranha in the aquarium literature,

Head of wimple piranha, Catoprion mento, *showing the extremely prognathic lower jaw and some of the specialized teeth. This species is included within the subfamily Serrasalminae, but it is not a true piranha.*

An Orinoco red-bellied piranha, Pygocentrus cariba *(lower), and a Manuel's piranha,* Serrasalmus manueli *(upper).*

it is a beautiful fish that has so far been seldom imported into the United States. In many books and manuscripts, photographs of both *S. piraya* and *S. cariba* are often mistakenly identified as *S. naterreri.* This has led to much confusion.

The genus *Catoprion* includes only one species, *C. mento,* the wimple piranha. Not closely related to the other piranhas, it was formerly placed in a subfamily of its own by the characin authority Dr. Jacques Géry. This fish has an extremely prominent lower jaw armed with very peculiar tuberculate, everted teeth that are spaced apart and not interlocking. It feeds mainly upon the scales of other fishes that are scraped from their bodies by these out-curving teeth. Adults also show an extended and almost filamentous dorsal fin. *Catoprion* should not be considered a "true" piranha, and in evolutionary terms can be considered the sister species to all the other piranhas. I am including it in this book because of its popularity, uniqueness, superficial resemblance to the real

piranhas, and the fact that its common name includes the title of piranha.

Senses

Hearing: Piranhas have acute hearing. An organ called the labyrinth is located within the skull and contains the inner ear as well as an organ that controls balance. The swim bladder acts as a resonator and amplifier of sound waves traveling through the water. The Weberian apparatus then transmits these sound waves to the ear. As mentioned earlier in the discussion of piranha classification, the Weberian apparatus is a chain of three small bones connecting the inner ear with the swim bladder.

Sight: The eyes of fish have a flat cornea and a rigid lens. The eyes of piranhas are best adapted for seeing in daylight, but may also possess a reflective layer on the retina that can enhance their night vision. This structure is similar to that of many other nocturnal animals such as cats and deer. (It is responsible for the characteristic eye-shine of these mammals when they are caught in the beam of a headlight.) Piranhas have excellent color vision and may be able to perceive a wider range of colors than humans. In common with all fish, there are no eyelids. (It should be mentioned that sharks and ocean sunfish possess a nictitating membrane, often referred to as a third eyelid.) Located on the side of the piranhas' head, their eyes have a very wide lateral expanse of vision but a limited anterior stereoscopic field. At rest, the eyes of piranhas are very nearsighted, but the lens can be moved forward and back by special muscles, permitting them to focus on more distant objects.

Smell: The paired nostrils are located on the dorsal surface of a piranha's head just posterior to its mouth. Each nostril or nasal pit consists of two openings separated by an easily seen flap of skin. Water entering the nostrils flows past a highly sensitive and much folded olfactory membrane. Special smell receptors in this membrane are connected with the portion of the brain that perceives smell. Experiments have shown that piranhas have an amazingly acute sense of smell, which greatly aids them in locating food in the often murky waters of their native habitat.

Taste: Piranha taste buds are concentrated within the mouth and pharynx, with a lesser number distributed on the lips. Many fish also have taste buds on their fins and bodies. Fish are not thought to have a particularly well-developed sense of taste, but we have all seen them quickly spit out a potential food item that is not to their liking.

Lateral line: The lateral line is a sensory organ found only in fish. It can be clearly observed as a thin line of small pores on the mid-sides of piranhas extending from the rear of the gill

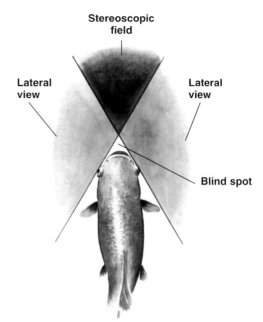

Piranhas' field of view is very wide, but due to the location of their eyes, they have very limited steroscopic vision.

plate to the tail. Under the scales of the lateral line is a canal filled with a jellylike substance and many sensory cells called neuromasts. This organ not only detects vibrations traveling through the water, but the direction of water currents as well. It is sensitive enough to respond to the pressure waves produced by the swimming or struggling motions of other fish. It can also detect the reflected pressure waves produced when the fish approaches an object. The lateral line organ is definitely an important navigational aid, being of particular importance during darkness or in turbid water. It is also useful in helping piranhas locate their prey.

The Piranha in Nature

Distribution

Piranhas are native only to the tropical portions of South America east of the Andes Mountains. The Amazon is the largest river draining this vast region. It is the world's greatest river, flowing over 4,100 miles (6,700 km) in an easterly direction across South America. It originates from a small spring on Mount Huagra in the high Andes of western Peru, eventually entering the Atlantic Ocean as the mightiest river on earth. Through its 200-mile- (322 km) wide mouth flows 20 percent of all the river water on earth! Ocean-going vessels can travel over 2,300 river miles (3,703 km) up the Amazon to the port city of Iquitos, the world's furthest inland port. Over 1,000 other rivers flow into the Amazon. Its largest tributary is the Rio Negro, which disgorges at its mouth a volume of water equaling

that of the second largest river in the world, by volume, the Zaire (formerly called the Congo). Within the Guiana Highlands of southern Venezuela, the Brazo Casiquiare connects the headwaters of the Rio Negro with those of the Venezuelan Orinoco. All these rivers are home to a rich assortment of piranha species. Various species of piranhas are also found within the smaller rivers and streams of the Guianas east of the Orinoco.

Other major rivers that support populations of piranhas are the Sao Francisco of eastern Brazil, and the Paraná and Paraguay. The latter two originate in southern Brazil, flowing south through Paraguay, and eventually enter the Atlantic Ocean via the Rio De La Plata near Buenos Aires, Argentina.

Piranhas' intolerance to cold is the major limiting factor to the southern extension of their range. Large winter kills of red-bellied and other piranha species are regularly reported from the middle and lower reaches of the Paraguay River south of Asunción, Paraguay, where winter air temperatures regularly drop below 40°F (4.4°C).

The Natural Environment

Contrary to the generally held belief among aquarists, the waters of Amazonia and the Orinoco drainage of Venezuela are not all soft and acid. Three distinct types of water are found within this area, each having its own unique set of characteristics resulting from differences in their origins. They are referred to as whitewater, blackwater, and clearwater. These distinctions often blur as waters of different types mix at the junctions of streams, rivers,

The Llanos savanna area of Venezuela, pictured here during high water, drains into the Orinoco River.

and lakes, and during times of seasonal flooding. Many species of fish prefer or are limited to a certain type of water. This is particularly true for blackwater forms. Knowing these preferences is often important for keeping and breeding them successfully in captivity.

Whitewater

The main channels of rivers originating in the mountains of the Andes carry an enormous load of eroded silt and sediment. This great amount of suspended and dissolved material imparts to these waters a tan or khaki-colored turbidity similar to the color of creamed coffee. Although relatively rich in nutrients, the opacity of these waters prevents the penetration of light required for the growth of submerged plants and photosynthetic plankton. The shoreline and bottom of whitewater rivers is made up of thick layers of mud created as the suspended matter settles to the bottom. Characteristic of these whitewater rivers is the extensive development of floating plant communities and the presence of dense growths of emergent shoreline vegetation.

The Amazon, Napo, Madeira, Purus, and Jurua are among the best-known of the whitewater rivers. These waters are moderately soft and close to neutral in pH. Depending upon the season, my own tests of the Napo and Amazon near Iquitos, Peru, showed a hardness range of 80 to 120 ppm (parts per million) and readings between 6.7 and 7.3 on the pH scale. Whitewater, being richest in nutrients of the three different water types, is the most biologically productive, with the greatest numbers and species of fish (including piranhas).

Blackwater

Rivers and streams originating in swamps and forest lowlands carry minimal amounts of suspended material. These rivers are transparent but stained a color resembling strong tea

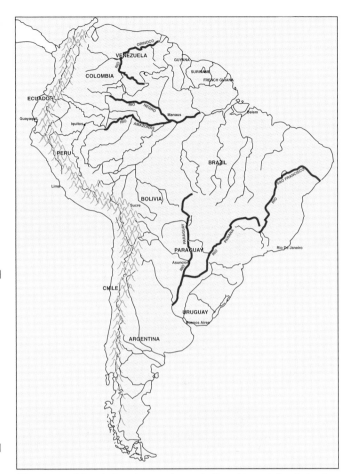

The rivers of South America are home to the wide variety of piranha species.

or cola from the tannins produced by the decay of leaves and other vegetation. The sandy soils of these regions are extremely acidic and retard the breakdown of humic acids in the litter, which permits the tannins to leach into the streams. The shores of these blackwater rivers are not muddy but resemble white sand beaches. The largest and most famous of the blackwater rivers is the Rio Negro of Brazil. Near Manaus, where this river joins the Amazon, the mixing of the waters of

Main channel of Amazon River upstream from Iquitos, Peru. The Amazon is classified as a whitewater river.

4.5; readings as low as 3.2 have been recorded from the upper Rio Negro. These waters are some of the purest on earth—extremely soft and usually with low levels of dissolved oxygen. Because of the lack of nutrients, plankton and insect larvae are found in very small numbers. This, combined with the low oxygen levels, results in a much smaller fish density than that of whitewater regions. Much of the food for nonpredatory blackwater fish comes from sources outside of the rivers such as terrestrial insects, forest vegetation, and fruits. Partly due to the smaller food base, piranha numbers are lower in blackwater habitats than whitewater ones. The species present tend to travel singly or in small, loosely organized groups and not large schools. It appears that the different water types are preferred by different species of piranhas.

these two great rivers is a famous tourist attraction. For a distance of nine to twelve miles (14.5–19 km) down-stream, the water is divided into two colors until blending is fully accomplished.

Blackwater is extremely poor in nutrients and highly acidic. The pH commonly ranges from 5.5 down to

Clearwater

Clearwater rivers arise in areas such as the Brazilian and Guiana highlands that are geologically very old. These areas have been so thoroughly eroded that little is left in the remaining resistant layers to dissolve or be washed away. These clearwater rivers tend to be very transparent, often appearing to have a blue or green cast. They lack the tannins and humic acids that are typical of blackwater. Nutrient levels are higher than that of blackwater but much lower than that found in whitewater. The excellent light penetration of these clearwater rivers encourages a lush growth of submerged vegetation. Their pH ranges between 6.0 and neutral. Clearwater supports an excellent population of fish. Small species are particularly abundant, finding food and protection within the aquatic vegetation. The Xingu, Tapajos, and Tocantins are examples of clearwater rivers. Piranhas are quite common in these habitats, exploiting the large prey base.

The soils of whitewater floodplains are comprised of thick layers of rich muddy sediments that are deposited yearly by the rivers during high water. Rio Napo, Peru.

Seasonal Changes

Rainfall in the Amazon Basin averages between 60 and 120 inches (150–300 cm) annually, but does not fall uniformly throughout the year. This, combined with the seasonal precipitation in the Peruvian and Ecuadorian Andes and other highland areas results in great seasonal fluctuations in the water levels of the region. Seasonally inundated floodplain forests are a characteristic of the Amazon rain forest. The productivity of the region is largely the result of this yearly rise and fall of the rivers combined with the year-round warm temperatures. The larger rivers undergo annual water level fluctuations of 20 feet to over 50 feet (600–1,500 cm). The whitewater floodplain forests are referred to as *várzea,* or *tahuampa;* those of blackwater rivers are known as *igapó.*

As the Amazon and other whitewater rivers rise, their turbid nutrient and mineral-laden waters overflow their banks, refilling the floodplain lakes and flooding the forests for many miles inland. The calm sun-heated waters of these lakes slowly clear as the suspended sediments gradually settle to the bottom. The combination of increased light penetration and the high nutrient levels results in an abundant growth of plankton. Fish enter the flooded forest and swim among the trees, feeding heavily upon the abundant insects, fallen fruit, seeds, and detritus. Although the seasonal flooding of blackwater rivers does not bring with it this influx of enriching nutrients, it does permit the fish to enter the previously dry forested areas. Having access to the nutritious food items within the forest is essential for the survival of the fish populations of these nonproductive waters. Many Amazonian fish, including piranhas, time their breeding season to coincide with the beginning of the rise in water levels and its associated abundance of food.

This is the blackwater Rio Tacshacuraray, near the Peruvian village of the same name. This river flows into the whitewater Rio Napo. Blackwater rivers lack the suspended sediments of whitewater areas, but are tannin-stained and acidic.

It is well known that most rain forest soils are very poor, having been leached of their nutrients by millennia of heavy rainfall. The only truly fertile soils of Amazonia are located in the floodplains of whitewater rivers. Their fertility is a

The soils of blackwater regions are sandy and firm, lacking the muddy nature of whitewater floodplains.

The most dramatic mixing of a blackwater and whitewater river is at Manaus, Brazil, where the blackwater Rio Negro meets the Amazon.

result of the yearly deposition of the rich sediments eroded from the Andes Mountains. Unfortunately, much of these *várzea* areas are being heavily exploited by logging operations or cleared for farming and the expansion of villages. The impact of this destruction upon the multitude of aquatic and terrestrial species dependent upon these seasonally flooded forests remains to be seen.

A clearwater tributary of the Rio Dimini in northern Brazil.

Natural Diets of Piranhas

The common perception is that piranhas are all voracious, obligate, flesh-eating carnivores, but many scientific studies involving direct observation in the field combined with detailed analyses of the stomach contents of freshly caught piranhas has shown this to be erroneous. Many species have yet to be thoroughly studied, but it is becoming increasingly clear that most are omnivorous opportunists, their diets varying according to their species, age, the season, and food availability. It is also becoming apparent that piranhas of different genera specialize in different foods. This may help to explain how in most regions within the piranhas' range many different species of these fish are able to coexist. With each exploiting different prey items, direct competition is minimized.

Very small juvenile piranhas of all species under four-fifths of an inch (20 mm) in length feed mainly upon planktonic organisms and microcrustaceans, adding small insects to this diet as they grow. By the time young piranhas attain lengths of approximately one and one half inches (40 mm) most begin to feed heavily on the fins of other fish. With increasing size, differences in the food preferences among the various genera become well developed.

The three *Pygocentrus* species tend to omit the fin-eating stage and at an early age begin to specialize in sheared off pieces of fish flesh and whole smaller fish. In adulthood, all three red-bellied piranhas remain voracious predators of other fish, varying this diet with mammalian, bird, and reptile flesh as opportunities present themselves, but even the menu of these mainly carnivorous species includes a small vegetarian component.

Analyses of the stomach contents of both young and adults of the short-faced and relatively weak-jawed

Pristobrycon and *Pygopristis* species have discovered that they feed largely upon seeds, fruit, leaves, and other vegetable matter, plus the fins, flesh, and scales of other fish. The seeds often form the major component of their diet. It is interesting that fins and pieces of fish are swallowed without being chewed, but the seeds are first thoroughly masticated into fine bits in the manner of their vegetarian relatives, the pacus. Adult *Pygopristis denticulatus* are most commonly found in forest streams, where fruits and seeds are readily available.

Smaller subadult specimens of most of the numerous *Serrasalmus* piranhas also specialize in fish fins and seeds, but the fins form the greater proportion of their diets. This is a large and diverse group of piranhas. Although fish fins comprise the major food item for many species of *Serrasalmus* throughout their adult life, there are exceptions. The larger and more powerful species such as *S. rhombeus,* the black or red-eyed piranha, switch to a diet that emphasizes fish flesh, but still devour a considerable amount of fish fins with lesser amounts of seeds and fruit. The widespread elongate piranha, *S. elongatus,* and the diamond-shaped *S. irritans* from Venezuela are primarily fin and scale feeders. Within the serrasalmines, scale feeding is most highly developed in *Catoprion mento,* the wimple piranha. A few species of *Serrasalmus* piranhas appear to be primarily seed eaters, at least during high water periods, varying this diet with lesser amounts of fins, scales, and fish flesh.

Nutrient Content of Scales and Fins

Analyses of the nutrient content of scales have shown that they are more nutritious than one might expect. Scales and fins are both covered with protein-rich mucous and are 35 to 40 percent protein (dry weight). They are

A flooded forest along the Rio Tacshacuraray, Peru. The waters of this area will be much deeper as the rainy season advances.

also an excellent source of calcium, a mineral often lacking in the soft acid waters of the region. Although not as nutritious as whole fish or fish flesh, fin feeding permits piranhas to exploit species that are too large to swallow whole or to be eaten by other predatory fish of similar size. Scales and fins can also be considered a renewable resource, being rapidly regenerated.

This banyan tree clearly shows the high water mark from the previous wet season. A residual floodplain lake can be seen in the distance. Peruvian Amazon.

A Pristobrycon *species* (striolatus?) *under one inch (2.54 cm) in length. At this size, piranhas of all types feed heavily upon micro-crustaceans and aquatic insects. Rio Apayacu, Peru.*

This exploitation of a rapidly renewable food source without eliminating it can be compared to the cropping of grass by grazing animals. When, and where, prey items are scarce, such as in the relatively fish-poor waters of the Rio Negro and other blackwater regions, this fin-feeding habit is a very efficient use of a limited resource and possibly essential to the piranhas'

A young black piranha, S. rhombeus. *As this young fish matures, its diet will switch from mainly fins to fish flesh and entire small fish. Rio Napo, Peru.*

survival. It is particularly interesting to note that the voracious red-bellied piranhas, which travel in large loosely organized groups and feed almost exclusively upon fish flesh, are often scarce in blackwater regions where fin-eating *Serrasalmus* species are commonly abundant. I have already mentioned that piranhas are not adverse to including dead food items in their diet and are efficient opportunistic scavengers.

It has long been known that vegetarian species of animals have longer intestines than strictly carnivorous forms because of the greater difficulty and time required to digest plant material. Recent studies by Dr. Leo Nico have shown that relative intestinal lengths of the different piranha species correlate very well with what we know about their diets.

Behavior in the Wild

Piranhas often travel in small, loosely organized groups. Exceptions are the scale feeders and the highly predacious *Pygocentrus* species. Scale feeders, such as the wimple piranha and *Serrasalmus irritans,* are almost always solitary hunters, while the *Pygocentrus* piranhas often travel in larger groups. Whether living in small or large groups, piranhas appear wary and suspicious of each other. Violation of an individual's personal space often leads to threat displays or aggression, which may take the form of head-to-tail circling, side-by-side body wagging, or chasing. It appears that they become particularly edgy when approached from the rear.

When Active

Piranhas are primarily active during the daylight hours. Adult specimens of the more predatory forms are most active at sunrise and late afternoon, retiring to sheltered resting areas during midday. From these retreats, one or two individuals may occasionally launch an attack at prey passing close by. Foraging by the other species and young individuals is more evenly distributed throughout the day.

At night most piranhas of all species rest quietly among plants or in other protected areas. Raiding of gill nets by piranhas during the hours of darkness has been reported, but I have never caught a piranha of any species while fishing at night.

Hunting Methods

Underwater observations by biologists in the Pantanal region of Brazil have discovered that piranhas utilize a variety of hunting methods. These include techniques of ambush, stalking, approaching under guise, and active chases. It is a fair assumption that piranha species in other regions employ similar tactics.

Ambush: Many types of piranhas have been observed dashing from cover in an attempt to ambush their prey. This may be performed by a single individual or a small group. Depending upon the species of piranha, the ultimate goal of this attack may be a mouthful of scales or fin, a piece of fish flesh, or an entire fish.

Stalking: When stalking, piranhas invariably approach their prey stealthily from the rear. Piranhas appear to be very good at evaluating potential prey. Favorite targets are fish engaged in other activities, such as feeding, courting, or fighting, which help distract their attention from the approaching predators.

Approaching under guise: Red-throated piranhas (*S. spilopleura*) have been observed using a very sophisticated hunting strategy: Instead of actively attempting to stay out of sight of their selected target, they openly linger in full view without showing any apparent interest. Ever so slowly they edge closer without alarming their prey.

Only at the very last minute do they dash forward to clip off a piece of fin.

Active chases: Small groups of piranhas may also openly approach and charge schools of other fish in an attempt to frighten them into scattering. Each piranha then singles out an individual specimen to pursue.

Whatever hunting technique is used, the tail region is usually the first part of a fish to be attacked. This should not be interpreted as a conscious effort on the part of piranhas to reduce their prey's mobility. It is rather the logical result of piranhas generally attacking from the rear, and the tail fin offering a large, conspicuous target.

Piranhas of all species are attracted to the feeding activities of other fishes or to those carrying prey. This may develop into a full-blown feeding frenzy where all species present are attacked. When more than one species of piranha is involved, they may even attack each other, resulting in fin predation and severe wounds.

"Aggressive Mimicry": The young of many piranhas up to a size of two inches (5 cm) are plain silver with a distinct black spot at the base of the tail. At this stage of their development they closely resemble many other characins of similar size, such as various species of *Astyanax, Moenkhausia, Poptella,* and *Tetragonopterus.* It has been proposed that this might be a type of "aggressive mimicry," permitting the piranhas to mingle with these potential prey species without causing alarm. At this size most piranhas feed heavily upon the fins of other fish. Being able to swim among their food supply during this period of rapid growth would be of great survival advantage.

Cleaners

A recently reported finding is that at least one species of piranha (*S. marginatus*) may act as a cleaner, removing parasites such as fish lice from the

This very small black piranha has just bitten out a portion from the tail of the young silver tetra, *Tetragonopterus argenteus.*

Plant Material in Diets

We must not forget that the diets of virtually all piranhas contain a percentage of plant material. This may include leaves, flowers, fruit, and seeds. Piranhas of many species have been regularly observed congregating beneath fruiting trees in the manner of pacus. In these situations Amazonian natives catch many piranhas on hooks baited with fruit. Depending upon the species of piranha and the time of the year, plant material may be the preferred dietary component. The presence of plant material in the stomachs of piranhas must always be carefully interpreted; in some cases it may have been accidentally taken while ingesting other prey.

Scavenging

Piranhas of all species are efficient scavengers, raiding gill nets, and devouring the dead carcasses of any species they encounter. I have personally observed at least three species of piranhas in the Rio Orosa of Peru feeding upon the bodies of fish killed as the result of temporarily low oxygen levels. This scavenging behavior directed at mammalian species, including humans, is largely responsible for the piranhas' undeserved reputation as savage and bloodthirsty maneaters.

bodies of larger piranhas. This is particularly remarkable because this piranha is normally a fin-feeding species that is avoided or driven off by other piranhas. The marine environment has many species of fish that act as cleaners, but this behavior in freshwater fish has been infrequently reported.

Defense Strategies of Other Fish against Piranhas

The presence of piranhas definitely affects the behavior and foraging patterns of other fishes, often limiting their open-water foraging at periods of high piranha activity. However, it is wrong to think that, except for persistent vigilance, other fishes have no defenses against piranhas. Defensive strategies employed by other fishes commonly reflect the piranhas' habit of approaching their prey from the rear and directing their attacks at the tail region. Upon the approach of piranhas, several

Serrasalmus marginatus, from the Paraguay and Piraná river systems, has been observed to clean external parasites from the skin of other piranha species.

24

species of cichlids, including the festive cichlid (*Mesonauta festivus*), may arrange themselves in a defensive ring with their tails to the center. While confronting the piranhas, the entire group slowly moves in the direction of cover. When bottom-dwelling species, such as the wolf fish (*Hoplias malabaricus*) and pike cichlids (*Crenicichla spp.*), sight piranhas, they have been observed to hide their tails in vegetation or laying it flat on the bottom. Some larger cichlids and freshwater "barracudas" (*Acestrorhynchus spp.*— really a characin and not related to barracudas) may actively repel piranhas with displays and assaults.

Many South American cichlids have large conspicuous markings at the base of their tails resembling false eyes. Well-known species include the peacock basses of the genus *Cichla,* oscars (*Astronotus spp.*), and some pike cichlids. Dr. Winemiller has proposed that these false eyespots may cause the tail region to resemble the head and therefore deter piranha attacks (see References, page 85). This may explain the proportionately less piranha damage seen on the tails and fins of these species compared to fishes of similar size that lack these markings.

The similarities of coloration and markings between young and subadult specimens of the red-bellied pacu, *Piaractus brachypomus* (*bidens),* to the red-bellied piranhas of the genus *Pygocentrus* has long been recognized and is most probably an example of protective mimicry. These flesh-eating piranhas normally do not prey upon similar-sized individuals of their own species. By resembling one of these piranhas, the pacu may possibly be protected against piranha predation while also gaining protection against attacks from other piscivorous species. Pacus eventually grow much larger than the piranhas, losing their credibility as mimics; it appears more

This tiger shovelose catfish, Pseudoplatystoma fasciatum, *was attacked by piranhas after being caught in a gill net.*

than coincidental that their coloration then changes to a dull brownish olive.

Breeding Habits

There have been limited firsthand observations of piranha reproduction in nature. Piranhas start to breed as the waters rise at the beginning of the rainy season. The native peoples of

A peacock bass, Cichla monomlus. *The false eyespot at the base of its tail is thought to cause the posterior portion of the fish to visually resemble its head. This may inhibit predation by piranhas that habitually approach their prey from the rear.*

25

The red-bellied pacu, Piaractus brachypomus (bidens), *below, closely resembles piranhas of the genus* Pygocentrus, *such as the red-bellied piranha,* P. nattereri, *above. This may afford them protection from attack by the piranhas. These two fish were caught within a few minutes of each other in the Rio Orosa, Peru.*

the region have long stated that these fishes prepare nests and guard their eggs. Until recently these stories were generally viewed with suspicion because such an advanced mode of reproduction was not expected nor consistent with what was known about characin reproductive biology. Eventually, direct observations, both in nature and in aquariums, proved once and for all that these reports were basically true, at least for the species so far studied. There is still disagreement about whether both parents, or a single parent, guard the nest, and whether this behavior is consistent within a single species. Further data might show that this behavior varies among the different piranhas.

After pairing and selecting a breeding area, piranhas prepare a nest to receive their spawn by biting off the plants and small roots close to their bases. A bowl-shaped depression is thus produced.

Courtship

The reproduction of most piranha species has not yet been documented in the wild nor achieved in captivity, but this is bound to change as field research continues and less commonly imported species become available. From what we know, courtship is often initiated by the male piranha actively pursuing females. The coloration of breeding piranhas may darken considerably, with larger *S. rhombeus, S. gouldingi,* and *P. cariba* turning almost black. Eventually, a pair selects a location among submerged vegetation or plant roots and begins to prepare the nest site. Both fish remove most of the vegetation from the chosen area by biting plants off near their bases. A hollow in the plants is soon created with a diameter approximately equal to the length of the fish. The pair actively protects the nest site and vigorously drives off others of their own kind. During courtship, both fishes often swim in tight circles above the nest.

Spawning

The details of the actual egg laying has only been fully observed in captiv-

ity. The breeding pair swims side by side above the nest with their abdomens touching. Periodically, this activity is punctuated by a quivering of both fish as the adhesive eggs and milt are deposited upon the plants.

Spawning is a protracted affair, often taking several hours to complete. Depending upon the species and the size of the breeders, from several

During the act of egg laying, the piranha pair swim in tight circles above their nest with their abdomens almost touching.

At the peak of the dry season rivers often become so low that they are non-navigable. This is the Orosa River of Peru during August 1995. The lack of water movement caused the dissolved oxygen levels to plummet, resulting in a major fish kill.

hundred to several thousand eggs are laid. The eggs of all species studied are approximately one-eighth of an inch (3.2 mm) in diameter. One or both parents vigorously guard the eggs and nest against other piranhas and fishes of similar size, but small fishes are unexpectedly not molested, even when they enter the nest to consume the spawn. This has also been observed in captivity. Hatching time varies from two to five days depending upon water temperature and possibly the species. The fry become free-swimming a few days later and seek food and shelter among thickets of submerged and floating vegetation. I have collected large numbers of piranhas under one inch (2.5 mm) in length in shallow lakes and slowly moving rivers among the roots of dense masses of floating water hyacinth (*Eichhornia crassipes*) and water lettuce (*Pistia stratiotes*).

Portions of these floating plant mats often break free and travel with the current for many miles, widely dispersing the fishes and other small species living within them. With ample food, piranhas grow quickly, studies in captivity indicating that they reach sexual maturity in one or two years.

Observations of red-bellied piranhas in Brazil indicate that members of this species may at times be gregarious breeders, with many pairs constructing nests in close proximity. They have also been observed to use the same spawning site in two consecutive years, raising the question as to whether some piranhas make short migrations to selected breeding areas.

Experiences with Breeding Piranhas in Captivity

Slight variations on this general mode of reproduction have been observed in captivity. In 1958 and 1959 *S. spilopleura,* the red-throated or diamond piranha, were bred at the Shedd Aquarium in Chicago in a 1,200-gallon (4,500 L) aquarium. This may very well have been the first captive breeding of any piranha species. An article documenting these significant accomplishments was written by William Braker, who was then the assistant curator, and appeared in the January 1960 issue of *The Aquarium* magazine. In this case the male drove the female off after spawning was completed and took sole charge of guarding the spawn.

Another commonly cited account is the 1966 article by Ledecky, which appeared in *Tropical Fish Hobbyist.* In this spawning the eggs were laid on the roots of floating plants(!). The pair ascended side by side to the surface, then turned upside-down to lay their eggs upon the vegetation. It is possible that the fish resorted to this strange behavior due to a lack of suitable rooted plant growth. I have been unable to find any other reports of piranhas spawning in this manner.

Another apparently nontypical reproduction of red-bellied piranhas occurred at the Shedd Aquarium in 1994. In this case the eggs were scattered about the nest and 1,200-gallon (4,560 L) tank with no significant nest guarding being performed by either parent. Once again, we have no way of knowing if this was an aberration of captivity or normal variation in the reproductive mode of this species.

During the summer of 1994, red-bellied piranhas were successfully bred at the Dallas Aquarium in Texas. Twenty-five adult red-bellies and several hundred neon tetras shared a heavily planted 2,000-gallon (7,600 L) display aquarium. The nest was constructed on a planted rock terrace in only 12 inches (30.5 cm) of water. Prior to spawning the breeding pair vigorously defended the nest site, with many of

their piranha tankmates suffering wounds and damaged fins. After egg laying, the female guarded the nest while the male patrolled the territory immediately surrounding it. There was no attempt made by either parent to keep the neon tetras from entering the nest and gorging themselves on the eggs. The breeding pair was quite old and many of the eggs were infertile. A portion of the spawn was removed to a separate aquarium for study. At a temperature of approximately 76°F (24.2°C) they hatched in a little less than four days.

In the spring of 1960 the Shedd Aquarium once again made piranha history when their black piranhas reproduced. An article by William Braker in the October 1960 issue of *The Aquarium* magazine documented this event in detail. In what appears to be typical piranha breeding behavior, the pair bit off the tops of all plants within their selected nesting area. Spawning was a protracted affair, taking almost four hours. Both parents diligently guarded the spawning site for three weeks. At 23 days the fry were approximately three-quarters of an inch (19 mm) long.

A series of black piranha spawnings, differing in some details from that at the Shedd Aquarium, was accomplished at the New York Aquarium during 1970. The single pair, housed in a 1,500-gallon (5,700 L) exhibition aquarium, was observed defending one corner of the tank. No nest-building activity was observed. Spawning took place in the late afternoon and early evening. The eggs were delivered in batches of 25 to 50 at two- to five-minute intervals over a period of three hours. The eggs were removed from the display tank and hatched in three days. The fry absorbed their yolk sacs by the ninth day and were free-swimming and feeding on live, newly hatched brine shrimp 24 hours later. At one year, the young had

Two species of piranhas are represented in this seine net catch; Pygocentrus nattereri, *the red-bellied piranha, and the more laterally compressed red-throated piranha, a member of the* Serrasalmus *"spilopleura complex." Amazon River at the confluence of the Orosa River, Peru.*

Additional particulars can be found in an article by Werner Schreiner and Douglas Kemper that appeared in the August issue of *Animal Kingdom,* the magazine of the New York Zoological Society. (For additional information on breeding, see pages 68–70.)

Natural Enemies

Adult piranhas have relatively few natural enemies. They are too large a prey for most fish-eating birds such as herons, egrets, and cormorants, and are given a wide birth by most diurnal predatory fishes. A small number are undoubtedly taken by caimans (species of crocodilians) and the increasingly rare river and giant otters. There are two unique species of freshwater Amazonian dolphins. It has been stated in the literature that the larger species, known as the pink porpoise or *boto (Inia geoffrensis),* has a particular fondness for piranhas. Within the piranhas' range live many species of large catfish. It is possible that these nocturnal predators surprise and devour an occasional piranha.

Young piranhas are fair game for many species of water birds, aquatic reptiles, and fishes. Their remains have been found in the stomachs of peacock cichlids and other large predatory fishes. They are also preyed upon by larger piranhas, including their own species.

Although it cannot technically be considered an enemy, the seasonal nature of the rainfall throughout most of the piranhas' range is responsible for many deaths. During the dry season, piranhas of all ages become stranded in dessicating lakes and ponds that are cut off from larger bodies of water. Many may die or become easy prey for predators and scavengers, including wading birds, vultures, and fish-eating mammals. This occurs most regularly in areas with a long and pronounced dry season, such as the Llanos region of Venezuela.

reached a length of two inches (50 mm). Of particular interest is that when some of the yearlings were returned to the display aquarium, they coexisted uneventfully with their parents.

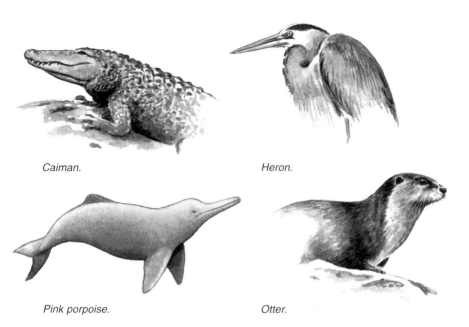

Caiman.

Heron.

Pink porpoise.

Otter.

Humans are undoubtedly the major predators of adult piranhas. In most parts of their range the larger piranhas are considered a desirable food fish. Large numbers are caught both deliberately and accidentally with gill nets, fish traps, and hook and line. At present, however, no piranha species appears to be threatened or severely declining in numbers and the chances of this happening are very improbable barring major unforeseen environmental disasters.

The Piranha Aquarium

Selecting the Aquarium

Three major criteria to consider when purchasing an aquarium for your piranhas are its shape, size, and construction. The most common design is the standard rectangular tank. So-called "show" tanks are similar, but taller compared to their length. Selecting the best design requires a degree of knowledge about aquarium biology and fish behavior.

The Role of Oxygen and Carbon Dioxide

Fish, like all higher life forms, require oxygen for respiration and produce carbon dioxide as a waste product of their metabolism. Inadequate levels of oxygen or excessively high concentrations

Although both these aquariums have the same capacity, the surface area is much less for the tall one.

of carbon dioxide dissolved in the water are fatal to most fishes. Although live aquatic plants utilize carbon dioxide during photosynthesis and produce oxygen as a byproduct, these reactions are inadequate to maintain fish life within the confines of an aquarium. The vast majority of the dissolved gases, including oxygen and carbon dioxide, enter and leave an aquarium through the water's surface. The larger the surface area of an aquarium in relation to its capacity, the more rapidly this gas exchange will occur. Contrary to popular belief, the major portion of the increased dissolved oxygen levels resulting from the use of air stones is not due to direct absorption from the bubbles. It is the increased circulation produced at the water's surface by the mechanical action of the rising stream of bubbles that is responsible for this beneficial effect.

Shape

When selecting an aquarium, always take into consideration the number, size, and behavior of the fishes you wish to keep. Obviously, larger fishes require roomier quarters, but behavioral needs must also be considered: Open water species that are active and tireless swimmers, or those that establish and defend individual territories, require more room than more sedentary or social species. Although piranhas are not unusually active fishes, many are quite territorial and tend to persecute each other when not given adequate room to disperse. Fish territories rarely incorporate much vertical space. By choosing an aquarium with as large a surface area as possible without unduly sacrificing appearance, you can maximize the ability for gas exchange while also providing needed room for the establishment of territories. I feel, therefore, that the standard rectangular aquariums incorporate the ideal proportions. Exceedingly tall tanks do not have enough surface or bottom area and their depth complicates cleaning and servicing.

Note: Drum bowls, once so popular for housing one or two small goldfish, should never be thought of as a permanent home for any fish, including piranhas. They do not hold enough water, and are nearly impossible to heat and filter properly.

Size

The larger the aquarium one can afford and has room for, the better. Their larger volume helps modify any sudden temperature or chemical fluctuations in water quality due to equipment failure or poor husbandry practices. Even though the piranhas offered for sale in aquarium stores are generally young and small specimens, it should not be forgotten that with good care they grow rapidly, soon reaching a considerable size for an aquarium fish. Always buy an aquarium that will be large enough to accommodate your fish when they reach adulthood. A 20-gallon (76 L) aquarium might be adequate to house a half-dozen two-inch (5.1 cm) piranhas, but 50 gallons (190 L) is the minimum size required for two or three adult red-bellied piranhas. If you cannot—or will not—make the commitment for an aquarium of at least this size, you should rethink your plans to keep piranhas.

Construction

The vast majority of aquariums sold today are of the so-called "all glass" construction. These are frameless with silicone cement used to hold the sections of glass securely together. The

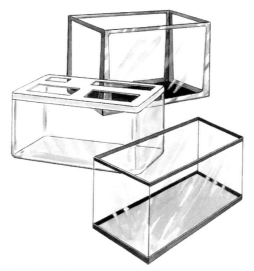

Aquariums of various construction are available. Here we see examples of the popular frameless all-glass, acrylic and metal frame styles.

larger the aquarium, the thicker the glass that is used. A decorative edging protects the upper and lower margins. Aquariums of this construction are attractive, durable, and readily available in many sizes.

Formerly, most aquariums were made with a frame of stainless steel or other metal. A tarlike putty held the glass walls in place and the bottom may have been glass or slate. These aquariums were very well constructed but heavy. I have always liked the appearance and durability of this type of aquarium. They are a good choice if you can find one, perhaps at a garage sale or from a friend who no longer needs it.

Aquariums are also made from acrylic. The major advantage of acrylic is its lighter weight compared to glass. They also have less tendency to crack as a result of accidental trauma. The disadvantages are their usually higher cost and the ease with which they become scratched.

Placement of the Aquarium

There are numerous factors that must be taken into consideration when selecting a location for your piranha aquarium. Among the most important are:

- the aquarium's weight
- its proximity to water sources and electrical outlets
- the aquarium stand
- natural light levels

Weight

One gallon (3.8 L) of water weighs 8.33 pounds(3.6 kg). A fully set-up 50-gallon (190 L) all-glass aquarium, complete with gravel substrate, rocks and other tank furnishings, and water, weighs at least 600 pounds (272 kg). Larger aquariums are proportionately heavier. This makes it imperative that you give careful thought to the placement of the aquarium and the construction of the stand that will support it.

The floors of many homes are not constructed to support such a massive

Various types of aquarium stands.

concentrated weight. It is common for apartment houses to limit the size and weight of aquariums permitted on upper floors. It is best not to place any large aquarium in the middle of a room where it would be located far from supporting architectural structures. Ground level or basement rooms are generally of stronger construction than upper floors and subject to less vibration. If you plan to purchase an unusually large aquarium, and the foundation of your home is anything other than slab construction, it is prudent to first consult a structural engineer.

The Aquarium Stand

Aquarium stands are available in many styles. Wrought iron stands are inexpensive, but are often rather unstable and not very attractive. Wooden stands, though more expensive than metal stands, can be very attractive. Many are of furniture quality, and provide cabinet space for pumps, motors, and necessary maintenance equipment. If you decide to buy a wooden stand, be certain it is constructed soundly and has a finish that is resistant to water.

Wherever you eventually choose to place your aquarium it is essential that it be perfectly level. This will prevent the formation of leaks due to uneven strains placed upon the joints of the aquarium. If your floor is warped or uneven it may be necessary to place shims under the aquarium's stand.

Utilities

An aquarium requires the use of lights, heaters, pumps, and motors. For convenience, it is essential that your aquarium be located close to electrical outlets. In addition, since regular maintenance will require periodic partial water changes, it is best if the aquarium is located within easy syphon-hose distance of a water source and drain.

Natural Light

For both aesthetic and husbandry reasons it is best not to locate an aquarium in front of a window; unless you place an opaque backing on the aquarium, the daylight shining through the tank will silhouette the fish, making it impossible to observe their attractive colors. It will also encourage the objectionable and excessive growth of algae, sometimes turning the water a very unattractive pea soup green. Summer sunlight can also cause the aquarium to overheat. It is best to depend upon an artificial light source for illumination; it can be controlled for duration, intensity, and direction.

Aquarium Equipment

Electrical Safety Concerns

Many of the necessary items of aquarium equipment require the use of electricity. We should never forget that the combination of water and electricity can be potentially hazardous. Always be certain to observe proper safety precautions. A few of the more important are listed below:
• Only purchase electrical equipment that has been tested and approved by the Underwriters Laboratory (UL).
• Read all operating instructions carefully and only use electrical appliances in the manner for which they were designed.
• Always use a ground fault interrupter device (available at pet stores and electrical supply houses). These will automatically turn off appliances plugged into them if they malfunction or develop a short circuit.
• Before servicing your aquarium, turn off or unplug all electrical devices.
• If you should ever experience an electrical shock when you touch the aquarium, its water, or appliances, immediately unplug all the electrical equipment until the source of this hazardous condition can be found.

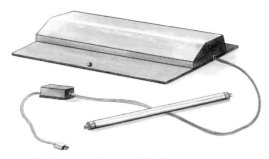

A typical full aquarium hood that incorporates a fluorescent light within a full tank cover.

• Promptly discard, or have repaired, any faulty piece of electrical equipment. Any repairs should be performed by the manufacturer or a professional electrician.

Light

The vast majority of aquarium light fixtures manufactured today are fluorescent. Some are incorporated in a full aquarium hood that also serves as a cover, preventing fish from jumping out, and slowing evaporation. Compared with incandescent light bulbs, fluorescent tubes are much more efficient. They give off significantly less heat, and produce more light per watt. To achieve the most natural appearance, it is important that a fluorescent bulb of the proper spectrum be selected. "Cool white" bulbs produce a pale, washed-out appearance in the aquarium, while so-called "grow lights," designed to encourage plant growth, impart an unnatural and peculiar pinkish-blue cast. To obtain the most natural and pleasing appearance, I recommend using bulbs labeled "full-spectrum" or "daylight."

Although standard aquarium light fixtures provide more than adequate illumination for viewing your aquarium, their light output is often not adequate to properly support the growth of live aquarium plants. This is particularly true

Aquarium heaters may be either fully submersible (left) or made to clip over the aquarium's rim (right).

if your aquarium is deeper than 12 inches (30 cm). If your taste includes natural rather than plastic plants, you might consider the purchase of an aquarium light fixture specifically designed for this purpose. These

An accurate thermometer is an essential piece of equipment. There are many models available, including those that attach with a suction cup to the inside of the aquarium (left), and others that attach to the outside glass of the aquarium by means of an ahesive backing (right).

incorporate either a number of fluorescent bulbs of different spectrums, or the high intensity light output of metal halide bulbs or specially designed VHO (very high output) fluorescent tubes. A less expensive solution can often be obtained by incorporating two, rather than a single, aquarium strip light to illuminate your aquarium.

Heaters and Thermometers

There are many excellent thermostatically controlled and adjustable aquarium heaters available. Some are suspended in the water from a clamp that attaches to the aquarium's top margin, while others are fully submersible. Submersible heaters are particularly suitable for homes where there are young children who might tamper with the exposed control dials of nonsubmersible types.

It is important to select an aquarium heater that is large enough to keep your aquarium at a uniform temperature. If your aquarium is located in a climate-controlled living space, a simple rule of thumb is to provide three watts of heat per gallon. A 50-gallon (190 L) aquarium would therefore require a 150-watt heater. Instead of using one heater of the needed wattage, many aquarists prefer two units, each providing one half of the required output. This slows the overheating of the aquarium if a heater's thermostat gets stuck in the "on" position, and slows the chilling if one heater should stop functioning.

A thermometer is essential for determining the temperature of your aquarium. Some are placed inside the aquarium, while others adhere to the outer surface of the aquarium's glass. I prefer one that can be attached to the front glass inside the aquarium by suction cup or a hanger where it can be readily observed. The stick-on outside types are often inaccurate when used on large aquariums with thick glass.

Many aquarium thermometers are very poorly made and highly inaccurate. Before purchasing one, check it against one you know to be accurate.

Air Pumps

The air pump is used to run air-driven filters (see pages 40–42) and air emitters or airstones. The vast majority of air pumps designed for the home aquarist are of the vibrator type, where a vibrating rubber diaphragm produces a flow of air. Aquarium air pumps come in a variety of sizes, the different models producing air of differing volume and head pressure. Many pumps produce a lot of air, but not enough pressure to pump the air to the bottom of deep aquariums. Before purchasing your air pump, discuss your needs with a knowledgeable pet store employee. It is also an advantage to obtain repair kits for the model you select as, with time, the diaphragms of vibrator pumps develop leaks and will require replacing.

Special note: An aquarium with proper filtration does not require additional airstones for aeration; the water circulation produced by the filter is more than adequate to assure the proper levels of gas exchange. It is also not necessary to purchase an air pump if your filters are motor driven rather than run by a flow of air (see below for information on filtration).

Filtration Processes

The subject of filtration is complex—entire books much larger than this one have been written about it. Therefore, I will try to summarize the most salient points to aid you in the selection of the proper filter system for your piranha aquarium. We will first discuss the theories of filtration, and then consider the various types of aquarium filters available.

There are three major and distinctly different types of filtration: mechanical filtration, biologic filtration, and chemical filtration. Many aquarium filters simultaneously perform more than one of these processes.

Mechanical Filtration

This is the easiest of the three types of filtration to understand. Simply put, mechanical filtration is the trapping of suspended particulate matter in the aquarium water by passing it through a filtering medium. (The trapping of dust in the filter of your home air conditioner is an example of mechanical filtration.) With time, the filter medium clogs and must be cleaned or replaced.

Biologic Filtration

The breakdown of fish wastes and uneaten food present in the aquarium produce organic compounds that are highly toxic to fish. Primary among these is ammonia. In the two-step process of biologic filtration, two major types of nitrifying bacteria break down the ammonia first into nitrites and finally into the relatively harmless nitrate ion. This process is known as *nitrification.* These beneficial bacteria can grow on any substrate in the aquarium. In a biologic filter we maximize this effect by providing a volume of some inert material with a large surface area where these beneficial bacteria can colonize. The nitrate produced can be utilized by plants as a fertilizer, but the major method of disposing of the accumulation of this chemical is by performing periodic partial water changes (see Aquarium Maintenance, pages 62–63).

Special note: Ammonia is much more toxic to fish when the water is alkaline (above pH 7.0). Under acidic conditions the ammonia is present in the much less harmful ammonium ion. It is therefore a good idea to keep a newly set-up piranha aquarium slightly on the acid side of neutral during the first few weeks as biologic filtration becomes established. This would be good for the piranhas in other ways also, since in nature they are generally found in neutral to rather acid conditions.

Chemical Filtration

In chemical filtration a chemically active substance is used to remove many non-ammonia pollutants from the water. These include dyes, proteins, heavy metals, growth-inhibiting substances, and many medications. The most commonly utilized chemical filtration medium is activated carbon. With time, the carbon loses its activity and must be replaced. Contrary to some older reports, there is no practical method of cleaning and reactivating this material at home.

Filter Types

Aquarium filters can be divided into two major categories: those that require

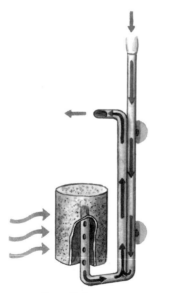

A sponge filter,. Air is pumped into the filter (top), mixes with the water entering the sponge block (bottom), and the aerated water exits the tube (center).

a remotely located air pump for operation, and those that have their own self-contained water pump. With the exception of the so-called powerheads, motor-driven types are located outside the aquarium—water is either pumped or syphoned into the filter and then returned to the aquarium by a passive overflow system or water pump.

Air-driven Filters

The principle of the air-driven filter is that a stream of bubbles directed through a lift tube produces a suction that draws water up into the tube and delivers it out through the top. This is often referred to as the air lift principle. The lift tube can be incorporated into filters of various designs, all directing the flow of water through a filtering medium before it enters the lift tube and is returned to the aquarium.

Sponge filters: Of simple construction and low cost, the sponge filter is a very good choice for a small aquarium or quarantine tank. Because they do not trap very small fish the way many power filters do, the sponge filter is particularly useful when raising baby fish. It is basically a block of sponge or foam attached to an air lift tube. Water is mechanically filtered as it passes through the sponge material. The sponge filter is also an efficient biologic filter. The many tiny pores within the foam block provide considerable areas for colonization by beneficial bacteria and the constant flow of water supplies them with the oxygen they require for survival. Well-established sponge filters can also be temporarily used in newly set-up aquariums to "seed" them with these beneficial microorganisms. Their main disadvantage is that they are hard to disguise in an aesthetically decorated aquarium and are most suited for use in smaller tanks without any other form of filtration.

Sponge filters are easily cleaned by removing them from the aquarium and rinsing them under a stream of water. To avoid destroying their biologic activity, one should use water that is the same temperature as the aquarium and not overly clean the filter.

Inside box filters: Also referred to as corner filters, these are basically small plastic boxes that house the filter media and are fitted with removable perforated covers. Inside the boxes are filter plates and standard air lift tubes that are connected to an air pump via a section of air line tubing. These filters are very inexpensive, and come in a variety of sizes and styles. If the correct size is selected, these box filters can provide adequate filtration for a small to medium-size aquarium.

During operation, water is drawn into the filter through the perforated top, passes through the filtering material and filter plate, and exits via the lift tube. The most commonly used filtering materials are a flosslike substance used in conjunction with activated carbon. The floss and carbon both serve as mechanical and biologic filters, with the carbon also providing chemical filtration.

Cleaning these filters involves removing them from the aquarium and rinsing or replacing the filter medium. To maintain the biologic activity of the filter, it is recommended that the aquarist not replace both the carbon and floss at the same time. It should be remembered that the ability of the carbon to act as a chemical filter diminishes with time, and must be periodically replaced. Medications and dyes used in the treatment of fish diseases can be efficiently removed from an aquarium by the temporary use of a box filter filled with activated carbon.

Undergravel filters: Undergravel filters are possibly the most popular filter for use in the home aquarium. If properly installed and regularly serviced they provide excellent mechanical and biological filtration for aquariums of virtually any size. They are also inexpen-

Box filters filled with both floss and activated carbon can provide complete filtration but, being of limited capacity, they are only suitable for smaller aquariums.

sive, inconspicuous, and not aesthetically intrusive. Their design consists of a perforated plastic filter plate that covers the bottom of the aquarium, and one or more associated air lift tubes.

The undergravel filter. This is probably the most commonly used filter for the home aquarium. When properly installed and serviced, it is an excellent mechanical and biologic filter suitable for any size fish tank.

HOW-TO:
Setting up the Aquarium

The first step in setting up your piranha aquarium is placing it in its permanent location. Due to their weight, moving aquariums after they are set up is very difficult and often results in the development of leaks or even cracking of the glass. As mentioned before, always make certain that the tank and its stand are perfectly level. To achieve this, shims might have to be placed under the legs of the aquarium stand. An improperly leveled aquarium develops strains that can cause a seam to split and leak.

Aquarium

Following are step-by-step directions for setting up your piranha aquarium:

1. If an undergravel filter is to be used, it should be placed in the aquarium with the lift tubes

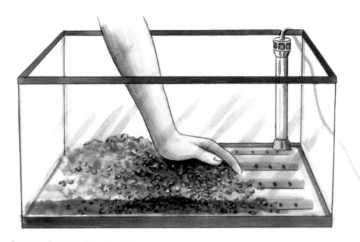

Step 1. Put the filter in place.

to the rear and covered with one and one half to three inches (3.8–7.6 cm) of washed aquarium gravel. (See Undergravel Filters, page 41.) If the undergravel filter is omitted, this depth should be reduced to not over one inch (2.54 cm). This lesser depth will help to prevent the development of harmful anaerobic conditions within the gravel.

Note: The gravel should not be so fine that it packs and prevents water circulation through it, nor so coarse that it serves as a trap for food and debris. The proper size gravel is available at all aquarium shops.

2. Place any rocks and bogwood in a way that creates an aesthetic appearance. It is often tempting to overdo the use of these furnishings. A pleasing and natural appearance will result if only one type and color of rock is used. Make certain the type of rock you select is safe for use in aquariums. Soft rocks that can easily be scratched with a knife often contain chemicals that are harmful to fish.

Note: Be certain that the rocks are placed so they rest securely on the aquarium bottom or filter plate. If simply placed on top of the gravel they may tip over, cracking the glass. To prevent the bogwood from floating, it should have been previously attached to a weight such as a piece of flat slate or kept submerged for a long

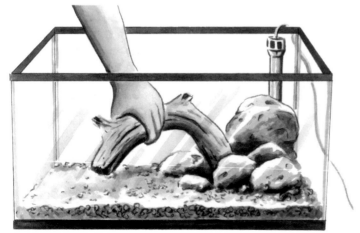

Step 2. Arrange the rocks and bogwood.

40

Step 3. Fill the aquarium with water to about two-thirds of its depth.

Step 4. Add plants, fill nearly to the top with water, and add the chlorine remover.

enough period of time to become waterlogged and lose its buoyancy.

3. Fill the aquarium approximately two thirds with water of the proper temperature—mid-70s to low 80s°F (24–31°C).

4. Any plants, whether living or plastic, can now be planted. In oder to create a pleasing effect, taller growing plants should be placed to the rear of the aquarium. Plants that grow from a crown should be planted so that the crown is level with the surface of the gravel. Complete the filling of your aquarium and add the chlorine/chloramine remover to the water. Be careful not to add the water so rapidly that it dislodges your plants or displaces the gravel.

5. Complete the set-up by installing your heater, thermometer, and any inside or outside filters (other than the undergravel type). Make certain you properly set the thermostat on the heater.

6. Place the cover and aquarium light on the tank. Only

after all this is done should you plug in the aquarium's associated electrical appliances.

Note: If you have another healthy, well-established aquarium at home, you may wish to add a bit of its gravel or filtering material to your newly completed setup. This will "seed" your new aquarium with benefi-

cial nitrifying bacteria and speed the establishment of biologic filtration.

Adding Fish

Fish should not be added at this time. The aquarium should first be watched for a few days to ensure that everything is running properly. When you start adding the fish, do not fully stock a newly set-up aquarium all at once. With the biological filtration not well established, this could result in a fatal and rapid rise in ammonia and nitrite levels. Always stock a new aquarium with fish gradually over a period of a few weeks. Periodic checking of the ammonia and nitrite levels is highly recommended, especially if your water is alkaline in nature (see special note under Biological Filtration, page 39). Inexpensive test kits are available at your local pet shop.

Step 5. Install the heater and thermometer and adjust the thermostat.

An outside power filter. Power filters come in a wide range of sizes and flow rates. It is easy to see when the filter materials require cleaning.

A one- to three-inch (2.5–7.5 cm) layer of gravel is placed over the filter plate and serves as the filtering medium. During its operation the aquarium's water is drawn through the gravel and filter plate and then returned to the aquarium via the lift tubes. Large

Cut-away view of a canister filter. Within each compartment of the filter a different filtering material can be used.

numbers of nitrifying bacteria are able to colonize the gravel, resulting in the entire filter bed becoming biologically active. Within limits, the greater the flow of water through the gravel, the greater the efficiency of the filter. There are special powerheads made that attach to the top of the lift tubes and greatly increase the flow rate. When powerheads are used to run an undergravel filter, an air pump is not needed.

When using powerheads to run an undergravel filter, either use them on all the lift tubes, or cap off the ones lacking them. The suction produced by a powerhead is so great that water will be pulled *downward* through uncapped tubes without a powerhead, bypassing the gravel filtering medium. Don't overdo the use of powerheads—unlike stream fish, piranhas are not comfortable in water with too much current or turbulence.

A potential problem of undergravel filters is that they tend to become clogged with debris. This reduces the flow of water through the gravel bed, which negatively affects the filtering efficiency. Specially constructed "gravel washers" are available that should periodically be used to vacuum the gravel of excess detritus. The use of gravel washers is discussed more fully on page 64, in the chapter on aquarium maintenance.

Power Filters

Like the air-driven filters, power filters are available in various designs. The three most common are the outside box-type power filter, the canister filter, and the trickle or wet-dry filter.

Power box filter: These outside filters conveniently hang from the rim of the aquarium. A motor is used to move the water from the aquarium and through the filter before returning it to the aquarium. The filtering media usually includes a combination of floss and activated carbon. These filters come in a variety of sizes and flow rates with models made to service aquariums up to 300 gallons (1,140 L) in size. They are a very good choice for the piranha aquarium, providing mechanical, biological, and chemical filtration. The filter medium is easily observed to determine when it needs cleaning, and its replacement is a simple matter.

Canister filters: These filters are located outside of the aquarium. Their motor pulls water from the aquarium through a length of flexible tubing into the canister. In this pressurized container the water is forced through a variety of filtering medias before it is returned to the aquarium via another section of flexible plastic or rubber hose. Due to their efficiency and large capacity, these filters are particularly suitable for larger aquariums. They can also be placed in a variety of remote locations both below and behind the aquarium or within a cabinetlike aquarium stand.

Canister filters provide complete filtration. As the filter becomes clogged with debris, the flow rate through the filter decreases. When cleaning a canister filter it is important not to replace all the filtering materials at the same time; to do this would temporarily destroy its biological filtration.

A disadvantage of the canister filter is its relatively high cost. Because it runs under pressure, it is essential that all fittings are properly secured after servicing and regularly checked to prevent leaks or floods.

Trickle filters: The trickle, or wet/dry filters, provide the most efficient biological filtration available for the home aquarium. After passing through a pre-

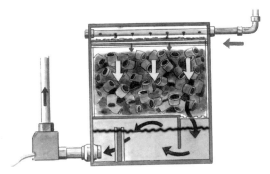

A trickle filter. Trickle filters provide extremely efficient biological filtration.

filter that removes particulate matter, water from the aquarium is trickled through a volume of an inert medium that serves as homes for nitrifying bacteria. It then can be directed through other filtering materials such as activated carbon before a water pump returns it to the aquarium. Because of their efficiency, trickle filters are particularly popular for aquariums that are heavily stocked or require particularly excellent water quality. Many aquarists consider them the filter of choice for marine fish and reef-type tanks.

Although trickle filters can be used with any size aquarium, they are particularly useful for filtering large volumes of water. Variations on this theme are used to maintain water quality in the largest public aquarium displays. They are also extremely efficient at maintaining high dissolved oxygen and low carbon dioxide levels in the water. Disadvantages of trickle filters are their high cost of purchase and their space requirements.

Obtaining Your Piranhas

Knowing the Law

If you are interested in keeping piranhas, the first thing to do is check with your local Fish and Wildlife Department about their legal status. In many states, the fear of accidentally or deliberately released piranhas becoming established in local waters has resulted in legislation forbidding their sale or possession. Exceptions may be made for legitimate scientific research or display at a public aquarium. The chance of piranhas being able to establish in the warm waters of our extreme southern states is a distinct possibility. It is a matter of record that a number of years ago a breeding population of piranhas was discovered in a Florida lake, necessitating the chemical removal of the entire fish population in that body of water. It seems a bit of an overreaction that many northern states, where piranhas could never survive in nature, also ban them. Whether or not you agree with these regulations, the fact remains that severe penalties have been established for anyone ignoring them.

Selecting Healthy Piranhas

Newly imported piranhas in dealers' tanks will almost invariably have portions of their fins missing due to aggressive behavior by others of their species. Piranhas are kept in rather crowded conditions by collectors, exporters, and importers. Crowding encourages fear and intraspecific aggression. When one realizes that young piranhas of most species—and adults of many—are primarily fin feeders, it is no wonder that so many of the piranhas offered for sale have their fins mutilated. Fins regenerate quickly; if the missing portions are not excessive and there is no sign of secondary infection, this alone should not discourage a potential purchase.

Use the same criteria in selecting your piranhas that you would use for any other aquarium fish. Healthy piranhas are active and alert, and feed readily. Avoid any fish that appear emaciated or sluggish. Excessive mucous production on the body or fins may be a sign of infection by external protozoans. Be certain there are no signs of labored respiration, which can indicate damaged gills, poor water conditions, or systemic illness (see Health Problems Diseases and Parasites, page 48).

Transportation

Piranhas of all but the smallest sizes are famous for their ability to bite through plastic fish bags, even when they are of double or triple thickness. The chances of this happening can be minimized if the fish are first mildly sedated with the tranquilizer known as MS-222. Unfortunately, not all aquarists have access or experience with this drug.

My recommendations are as follows: If you do not have too far to travel, I'd suggest the use of a plastic bucket to transport your fish. When longer travel periods are involved, I recommend that each fish be placed in its own snap-top plastic container in which you have previously poked a few holes. The container should be large enough for the fish to swim normally and is then placed in a larger plastic fish bag filled with an adequate amount of water to cover the container. The bag is then oxygenated and knotted or tied shut with a rubber band. The advantage of this set-up is that your fish have access to all the water and oxygen in the bag, without being able to bite through it. This method has been proven very successful in safely transporting piranhas (and spiny catfish and cichlids) to the United States from South America. Whichever method you employ, always transport piranhas one per container, as piranhas packed in groups often inflict severe damage upon each other.

Quarantine

It cannot be emphasized too strongly that all new piranhas—and all other fish for that matter—should undergo a quarantine period before being added to your aquarium. This not only helps prevent the introduction of potential pathogens, but also gives the new fish time to settle down and become adjusted to aquarium conditions and diets.

The quarantine aquarium must be of adequate size to accommodate the fish being treated. Tank furnishings need not be fancy—one or two large sponge filters, a heater, and a few rocks or pieces of bogwood to provide hiding places and give security are all that are needed. A light is not required, but a glass top will keep the fish from jumping out and help maintain a uniform temperature in the aquarium. This simple set-up permits ease of cleaning and rapid sterilization after use. The quarantine period should be a minimum of three weeks if no problems arise, but can be lengthened if conditions warrant. If

Piranhas can be prevented from biting through a plastic bag by first placing the piranha in a perforated container.

more hobbyists took the time to quarantine all their new fish, the incidence of diseases, parasitic infections, and unexplained deaths would be greatly reduced. Quarantines have long been required procedures for all species of animals at zoological gardens and public aquariums.

During quarantine the fish should be examined carefully at least twice daily. Make certain all specimens are feeding well, and promptly remove any uneaten food. At the first signs of trouble, appropriate treatment should be initiated. It is wise to treat all new fish for the presence of external flukes (see discussion on flukes, pages 53–54).

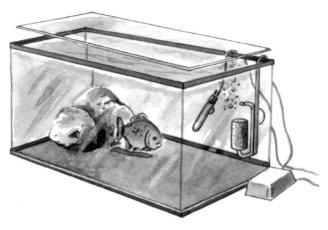

Quarantine or hospital aquariums need not be fancy. All that is required are a small filter, a heater, and simple furnishings to provide the fish with security.

A piece of aquarium airline tubing being used to slowly acclimate a piranha to the aquarium's water conditions. Note the use of a clamp to slow the flow of water.

Acclimatization

It is important that you gradually acclimate your newly purchased specimens to the water conditions of your aquarium; the chances are that they do not match those at the aquarium shop. Float the fish bags in your aquarium until the temperatures equalize. Then gradually, over a period of at least an hour, repeatedly add a little of the tank water to the fish bags. This will ensure that when you finally introduce your fish into the aquarium, they will not be shocked by drastic differences in pH or hardness. Another good method is to place your piranhas individually into plastic buckets of two- to five-gallon (7.6–19 L) capacity and, by the use of a piece of air line tubing, slowly let water syphon from the aquarium into these containers. A clamp can be placed on the tubing to prevent overly rapid addition of the tank water. Regularly check that the buckets are not overflowing.

Introduction into Your Aquarium

When quarantine is completed, it is time to introduce your new fish into their permanent home. Make certain that water temperature and chemistry of both tanks are as similar as possible. Net your piranhas singly to avoid the chances of them biting each other. To avoid damage to the nets from the their teeth, they can also be caught with wide-top jars.

Certain precautions need to be taken if your new specimens are being added to an established group. Most importantly, the piranhas in question must be one of the social species that tolerate being kept in groups. Piranhas have an excellent feeding response and are attracted to fish that appear disoriented or frightened, often immediately attacking a new fish that is added to their aquarium. This aggressiveness appears particularly well developed in the fish-eating *Pygocentrus* and fin-feeding *Serrasalmus* species. Some piranhas appear to have a fairly well-developed sense of territoriality and will often attack strange individuals. Also, the aggressiveness is greatly enhanced if the fish are in breeding condition or if they are hungry. Before adding your new fish it is therefore recommended that you first feed the piranhas in the tank that is to receive them and then turn off the aquarium light. Piranhas are diurnal feeders and the combination of having recently eaten and darkness should help calm any aggressive tendencies. By the next morning the new fish should have become adjusted and accepted by their tankmates; however, it is still wise to check during the next few days that all is going well. A few nipped fins is nothing to worry about; it may take a while until the newly added specimens are fully integrated into the group. It is never wise to attempt to mix specimens of significantly different sizes.

Health Problems, Diseases, and Parasites

One of the greatest challenges for the tropical fish hobbyist is the accurate and early diagnosis of problems affecting their fish. A complete discussion of aquarium fish diseases and illnesses is well beyond the scope of this book; this chapter is meant to serve as a primer to help aquarists prevent, recognize, and treat the maladies they are most likely to encounter. Unfortunately, not all the diseases and parasitic infections of fish can be positively identified without specialized laboratory techniques, but fortunately for the home aquarist, a relatively few illnesses make up the vast majority of the commonly encountered problems.

Prevention

Piranhas are quite hardy and adaptable, but even the most durable fish can fall victim to a variety of ills. It cannot be stressed too strongly that the best treatments start with prevention; an ounce of prevention *is* worth a pound of cure. Prevention should begin by the aquarist learning as much as possible about piranhas *before* purchasing them. This, combined with the careful selection of healthy specimens, followed by a three-week compulsory quarantine period are the most important steps an aquarist can take to avoid outbreaks of disease. During quarantine all fish should be observed daily for any signs of abnormality, and appropriate treatment should be promptly initiated as needed. With the exception of flukes (see pages 53–54), the author does not recommend the prophylactic use of medication for piranhas that are not demonstrating signs of illness. A quarantine period followed by consistently good husbandry techniques will help ensure that your piranhas live a long and healthy life.

Poor water quality reduces a fish's resistance and increases its susceptibility to disease. It can also cause symptoms that mimic an infectious disease. Whatever the symptoms, always check the aquarium's pH, ammonia and nitrite levels, and temperature before adding medication. Sometimes all that is needed is a partial water change.

Sensitivity to Medications

Serrasalmids in general are extremely sensitive to some of the most widely used fish pharmaceuticals such as Dylox® (also known as trichlorophon or Masotin®) and malachite green. Piranhas should never be exposed to Dylox, and malachite green should always be used at half the dose recommended for most other fishes. (This will be discussed more fully on pages 51, 53, and 56.)

The Hospital Aquarium

An important tool in the treatment of sick fishes is the hospital aquarium. It is particularly useful for the care of an injured fish or when a disease affects one or two specimens and is determined to not be contagious. When dealing with a highly contagious disease affecting most of the fishes in the aquarium, it is best to treat all the fishes in their original tank.

The water in the hospital aquarium should closely match that of the main tank. To reduce stress, lighting should be subdued, and some hiding places provided in the form of aquatic plants, rocks, or bogwood. A well-conditioned sponge or box filter completes the essentials.

Chemical Filtration

Activated carbon and many other types of chemical filtration absorb most drugs and medications from water. Always remove the carbon from your filter system before adding medications to your aquarium. At the end of the treatment a partial water change and the replacement of the carbon will eliminate the remaining drugs from the water.

Wounds

Probably the most commonly occurring ailment of captive piranhas are wounds, either of a very minor nature or life threatening. Wounds may be the result of aggressive interactions within a school of piranhas or accidentally inflicted secondary to panic. Understanding piranha behavior and taking proper precautions can avoid most injuries. It is inviting trouble to attempt to keep more than one piranha of the solitary fin- and scale-eating species in the same aquarium.

Fright Responses

Contrary to their undeserved reputation, piranha species are very shy and nervous fishes that are highly prone to an exaggerated fright response. This may be elicited by a stimulus as innocuous as the moving silhouette of a person passing between the aquarium and a brightly lit window. Attempting to net a piranha almost always results in a major commotion. Public aquariums often resort to fish tranquilizers before attempting to transfer adult piranhas from one tank to another. A severely frightened piranha dashes wildly about the aquarium seeking to flee from the source of its fear. The results are abrasions, split fins, and wounds as the piranhas collide with the aquarium's furnishings and its glass walls. Frightened piranhas have the nasty habit of indiscriminately snapping at any object they come in contact with. They do not differentiate between a fish net or one of their tankmates (or the aquarist!). This is even a problem when collecting piranhas in the wild. When a group of piranhas are captured in a minnow seine, their wildly snapping jaws not only may destroy the net, but invariably lead to mutilated specimens. Never attempt to net more than one piranha at a time! When servicing your piranha aquarium, take all the care needed to prevent them from panicking.

Treatment of Wounds

A minor wound of a healthy piranha, especially if it only involves the fins, usually heals uneventfully without treatment. Clean, well-filtered water that is low in dissolved organics is conducive to rapid healing and helps prevent the chances of secondary fungal or bacterial infections. It is another matter if the wound is severe. If you are keeping a group of piranhas together, you should promptly remove any severely injured specimen to the hospital aquarium. Piranhas often become cannibalistic on an obviously compromised tankmate.

Badly injured piranhas should be prophylactically treated with a broad-spectrum antibiotic to prevent infection. Commercially available nitrofurans used according to manufacturers' directions are some of the best. Products containing a combination of nitrofurazone and furazolidone are particularly effective. They are nontoxic to piranhas and do not destroy biologic filtration. These drugs also have the ability to be absorbed into the fish's body resulting in a therapeutic blood level, thereby

Bacterial Fin Rot: This disease can progress very rapidly, destroying the fins and killing the fish unless promptly treated.

fighting internal as well as external infections. A 50 percent water change is recommended after five days followed by a second treatment of equal duration. If no improvement is noted in three or four days, the bacteria involved may be resistant to this drug. Only then would it would be appropriate to try a different antibiotic. Before adding another drug, always remove the first with activated carbon and/or a large water change. It is never a good policy to experimentally mix antibiotics.

Tuberculosis is a very slowly progressive and contagious disease.

Untested arbitrary combinations of drugs can be very dangerous and result in fatal consequences.

Bacterial Infections

External Bacterial Infections
The most common causative factor in bacterial infections of piranhas is the secondary infection of injuries. Bacterial infections, whether of the fins or body, can usually be recognized by their red and bloody appearance and rapid tissue deterioration. Left untreated, the bacteria can spread throughout the bloodstream resulting in fatal septicemia (blood poisoning).

Fin Rot
Bacterial fin rot first manifests itself as a clouding or reddening of the fin edges. Left untreated, this rapidly progresses to severely frayed and destroyed fins. It may then spread to the body. Once it has reached this stage there is little hope for survival. Water high in organic waste products or extreme in pH levels are predisposing factors.

Bacterial infections of fish should be promptly treated with a broad-spectrum antibiotic. The regimen discussed under the treatment of wounds (page 49) should be followed.

Tuberculosis
Fish tuberculosis is a much more common disease of wild and domestic fishes than most people realize. This is because the lesions produced are most often found in the internal organs and not recognized unless an autopsy, which includes specialized tissue stains and microscopic examination, is performed. It is caused by *Mycobacteria marinum* and other related species. It is transmitted by ingestion of infected fish flesh or water in which the bacteria is present. Aquarists should be wary of diets comprised of live fish or uncooked

fish flesh. Symptoms of this disease are chronic and nonspecific in nature. Infected fish gradually lose weight, become listless, and often separate themselves from the rest of the group. The symptoms often reflect the organs affected; for instance, if the kidneys are badly damaged the fish may show pop-eyes and bloat due to an internal accumulation of excess fluids. The fish's color may be poor and small granulomatous lesions resembling pimples may appear on the body. These skin lesions, when present, are often observed at the fin bases and around the orbit.

Fish tuberculosis is most often a disease of the old and infirm. Since this disease is easily spread through cannibalism, it is wise to remove all obviously sick and dying fish prior to their death. There is no effective treatment and fish diagnosed with this disease should be humanely disposed of (see techniques of euthanasia, page 73). The causative organism is commonly found in soil and both freshwater and marine environments. The best prevention is to keep your fish in peak health through a combination of excellent nutrition, regular cleaning of the gravel, and maintenance of good water quality.

Although fish tuberculosis is not caused by the same organism that commonly affects humans, it can still be transmitted to us. Such infections are characterized by a chronic skin rash resembling small nodules, and are most often observed on the hands. People with compromised immune systems are most at risk. If cuts are present on the fingers or hands, rubber gloves should be worn for protection when servicing your aquarium.

Fungal Diseases

There are many internal and external fungal diseases that affect fish, but the two most common are body fungus and gill fungus.

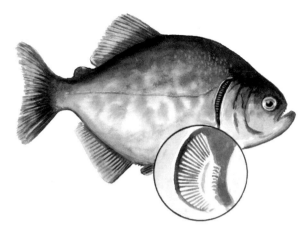

Gill rots, whether bacterial or fungal in nature, are very difficult to treat and may lead to death by suffocation.

Body Fungus

Body fungus is among the easiest of fish diseases to identify. It is caused by fungi of the genus *Saprolegnia* and related species. These are the same fungi that attack infertile fish eggs and dead fish. True external fungal infections resemble patches of fuzzy white or tan cotton wool or bread mold (which is also a fungus) appearing anywhere on a fish's body or fins. This fungus does not attack undamaged tissue, but secondarily invades the dead and dying flesh of wounds, injuries, and bacterial lesions. Once established on a living fish, the fungus spreads to healthy tissue by sinking rootlike hyphae into the fish's flesh. Fungus, being a plant, is unaffected by standard antibiotics. Malachite green is one of the most commonly used treatments for fungus; unfortunately, it is highly toxic to piranhas when used at the therapeutic dose required to treat this ailment. If caught early, body fungus can be successfully combatted by using common rock salt at the rate of

51

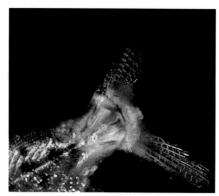

Fungus at the base of a piranha's tail secondary to being attacked by another piranha. The cotton-wool appearance of the fungal growth can be clearly seen.

one tablespoon per gallon (3.8 L). Piranhas tolerate this treatment well. Do not use marine aquarium salt mixes as they contain other chemicals and buffers that will alter the pH of the water. At this concentration salt will also kill many aquarium plants and snails. Adding two drops of 37 percent formaldehyde solution per gallon (3.8 L) to the salt bath is

A small wild-caught tetra parasitized by the larvae of a digenetic fluke.

helpful. The formaldehyde slowly dissipates, and a second addition should be made in three days. Nitrofurazone (not a true antibiotic) has antifungal properties and will also help prevent secondary bacterial invasion. In advanced cases of fungus the drug Griseofulvin used at a rate of 38 mg per gallon (10 mg per liter) as a long-term bath is recommended. This prescription drug must be obtained from a veterinarian.

Gill Fungus

Fungus of the gills, or *Branchiomycosis,* is a rather uncommon but highly contagious and dangerous disease that is quite resistant to treatment. The destruction of the gills interferes with the fish's respiration, eventually resulting in death by suffocation. Causative agents are injury to the gills initiated by high levels of organic pollution, toxic chemicals, or parasites. It is most commonly seen in newly imported fish where overcrowding and delays in shipping have resulted in severe fouling of their water. Symptoms include labored respiration, lethargy, and lack of interest in food. The diagnosis can be easily confirmed by carefully netting the fish and examining its gills for areas of inflamed and dying tissue. This disease is more easily prevented than treated. Carefully examining fish before purchase combined with the use of a quarantine tank and attention to water quality should prevent this disease from becoming established in your aquarium. Griseofulvin, used as recommended in the discussion of body fungus (page 51), may prove curative in the early stages.

Special note: Of very similar appearance, and equally dangerous, is the relatively rare bacterial gill disease. Since it is very difficult to visually differentiate one from the other, I recommend using a broad-spectrum antibiotic as part of the treatment whenever gill rot is observed.

External Parasites

External parasites come in many forms. These include worms (helminths), crustaceans, and protozoans. Some are large enough to be easily seen and identified, while others are microscopic in size. If you have no access to a microscope, diagnoses must be made based on symptoms, which is not always easy or without risk of error.

Flukes

Many species of helminths, or worms, are parasites of fish, but only a few are of concern to aquarists. The most important helminth parasites of aquarium fishes are the flukes. Flukes are parasitic trematode worms. They are classified as either digenetic or monogenetic, depending upon the number of host species they require to reach maturity.

Digenetic flukes are internal parasites that require one or two specific intermediate hosts to complete their life cycles. Depending upon the species of fluke, fish may be an intermediate or the final host. Intermediate stages may live as encapsulated larvae in many organs of the body. The adult digenetic fluke most often inhabits the digestive tract of its host. Eggs of the fluke are excreted along with the host's feces. Snails and small crustaceans are common intermediate hosts. Digenetic fluke infestations in aquarium fish are relatively rare and of little concern to the home aquarist.

Monogenetic flukes require only one host species for their full development. They are common and potentially serious parasites of aquarium fish. There are two main classes of monogenetic flukes that affect ornamental fishes: The dactilogyrids live mainly on the gills and are egg layers, while the live-bearing gyrodactylids parasitize the skin and fins. Both may be found on the same fish. Flukes attach themselves to their host by a hooklike haptor organ and feed on blood and tissue fragments. Unfortunately for aquarists, these flukes are too small to be seen without the use of a low-power microscope. In the confines of an aquarium flukes reproduce rapidly and are one of the most commonly unrecognized or misidentified causes of fish loss. Almost any species of fish, both wild caught and domestically raised, may harbor flukes.

Gill flukes have been documented on wild piranhas. Depending upon the severity of the infestation, symptoms may include "coughing" and "spitting" motions, breathing through one set of gills at a time, flared gills, reluctance to feed, and labored respiration. The damage to the gills interferes with respiration and may result in secondary bacterial and fungal infections.

Body flukes are often host specific and less likely to spread among different species of fishes; nevertheless, they can be a very serious problem. Twitching of fins, "scratching," and pinpoint-size red spots or streaks on the fins or body are signs of body flukes. In the more severe cases the fins become ragged, resembling bacterial fin rot.

It should be assumed that all newly purchased fishes are possible carriers of flukes. This is the one health problem I recommend treating during the quarantine period whether the fish shows symptoms or not.

Most fluke remedies available in pet shops contain the drug Dylox® (also known as Masotin® and Trichlorophon). *It is highly toxic to serrasalmine fishes and should never be used on piranhas.* This is really no great loss since many strains of flukes have developed a resistance to this medication. The drug of choice is praziquantel, also

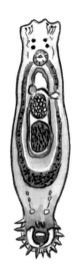

Gyrodactylid (left) and dactylogyrid (right) flukes. Flukes are a much more common and serious problem in aquarium fish than most hobbyists realize.

known as Droncit®. It must be obtained from a veterinarian, and is used as a two- to three-hour bath at a concentration of 10 ppm (38.0 mg per gallon [3.8 L]). Recent information indicates that 2 ppm (parts per million) for 24 hours is also effective. Praziquantel is rather expensive, and it is therefore advisable to use a container only as large as needed for the medicated bath. The fish should be removed, or the water changed, promptly after treatment. Praziquantel is used routinely by public aquariums on all new fishes, both freshwater and marine. Droncit does not destroy fluke eggs so treatment should be done *before* the fishes are added to the main aquarium. Live feeder fishes, particularly goldfish and bait minnows, are major carriers of both gill and body flukes. They should never be fed to piranhas unless first defluked.

Parasitic Crustaceans

The phylum Crustacea includes such familiar animals as lobsters, shrimps, and crabs. Unfortunately for aquarists there are also species that parasitize fishes. The two most commonly encountered are anchor worms and fish lice. Both are rare on wild imports and usually enter an aquarium via the vector of infected live feeder fishes. Since many pet shops use goldfish to feed their piranhas, it is wise to check all piranhas before purchase for the presence of these parasites.

Anchor worms are not worms at all, but copepod crustaceans of the family Lernaeide that are highly modified for a parasitic existence. Adults are approximately ¼ inch (7 mm) long and resemble toothbrush bristles embedded in the fins or under a scale. Their color can vary from white through shades of gray, tan, or green. What appears to be a forked tail is a pair of egg pouches. They have a complex life history and pass through a number of different stages. Only the adult female is a true parasite. Anchor worms can be difficult to eradicate. The drug Dylox® is normally used but, as previously mentioned, it is fatal to piranhas. Droncit, so useful in the treatment of flukes and other helminths, is ineffective against crustaceans. Formaldehyde used at two to three drops per gallon (3.8 L) is often recommended but its ability to fully eradicate this parasite is questionable. This leaves the aquarist the unpleasant alternative of sedating the fish and then manually removing the pests with a pair of tweezers or dabbing them with a small cotton swab dipped in alcohol. Often this will have to be done a number of times to fully eradicate these pests. There are a number of fish tranquilizers and sedatives on the market. The best and safest contain tricaine methanesulfonate (MS-222) as the active ingredient. Obviously, this can be time consuming and very stressful to the fish. There is also the hazard of the aquarist receiving a severe piranha bite. Avoiding the use of live feeder fish is the best way to keep this parasite out of your aquarium.

Argulus, or fish lice, are flattened, shield-shaped crustaceans that resemble a translucent tick. They measure between ⅛ and ³/₁₆ of an inch (4–12 mm) and attach themselves to their host with a beaklike stylet. The toxic substances injected by the louse when puncturing the fish's skin causes severe inflammation and local swelling. These wounds serve as points of entry for secondary bacterial and fungal infections. Like anchor worms, argulus most commonly enter the aquarium with contaminated live food. The treatment for fish lice on piranhas is the same as that for anchor worms and, as with anchor worms, they are more easily avoided than successfully treated.

External Protozoan Parasites

Protozoa are one-celled organisms. Many different species are common external or internal parasites of fish. Frequently encountered and potentially fatal fish diseases caused by protozoans are ich and the various blue-slime diseases.

Ich (pronounced "ick"), also known as white spot disease, is caused by the external parasitic protozoan *Ichthyophthirius multifilis*. It is extremely common and the first disease encountered by most new aquarists. Symptoms of ich are easily recognized, and it is just as easily cured when caught early. There is absolutely no reason for any observant and conscientious aquarist to lose fish from ich.

A fish with ich appears to have been sprinkled with the fine white grains of table salt or sugar. The small white spots are often first noticed on a transparent fin or a darkly colored portion of

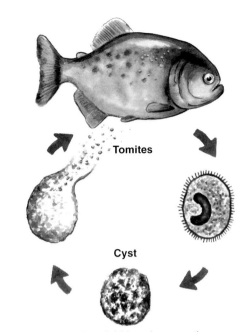

Life cycle of Ichthyophthirius, *the causative organism for ich.*

the body. Contrary to popular belief, these white spots are not the actual parasites, but the nodules produced by the host fish in an effort to wall them off. The protozoan is microscopic and too small to be seen with the naked eye. A fish with ich twitches its fins and repeatedly scratches itself against the aquarium furnishings in unsuccessful attempts to dislodge the parasites. Left untreated, the white spots increase rapidly in number, and may involve the gills and eyes. The fish becomes increasingly lethargic, and before death occurs, the skin and fins may actually slough in patches. When viewed under a microscope, the ich organism is unmistakable. The nucleus is light colored and C-shaped and the cytoplasm is granular and appears to be tumbling inside the cell.

Anchor worms on a goldfish. The forked "tail" is really its paired egg pouches. This is one parasite that is easier to prevent than treat.

A fish louse, Argulus sp. *Treatment is similar to that for anchor worms. A quarantine period for all newly purchased piranhas or feeder fish is the best means of prevention.*

Only a portion of this parasite's life cycle is spent on a fish. When the organism matures it leaves its host, settles to the bottom, and forms a cystlike structure. Within its capsule it repeatedly divides until there may be thousands of small cells. The cyst then bursts and the immature *I. multifilis* tomites swim through the water seeking a host fish. After accomplishing this, they then penetrate the outer layer of the skin, grow to maturity, and the cycle is repeated.

Slimy skin disease. Similar symptoms can be caused by a variety of different protozoans.

It is important to note that only in the free-swimming stage is ich vulnerable to treatment. Commercially available formalin/malachite green formulations are effective treatments. Because of piranhas' sensitivity to malachite green, these products should be used at half the recommended dosage and the fish carefully observed for signs of stress. It often takes two or three days before improvement is noticed. Treatment should be continued for at least five days after there are no longer any signs of disease. Raising the water temperature to 80°F (27°C) will speed up the parasite's life cycle and shorten the treatment period. A cure is usually accomplished within 10 to 14 days.

Other treatments that have been used more in the past for ich are mercurochrome and quinine. Mercurochrome was used at a rate of three or four drops of 2 percent solution per gallon (3.8 L). It is now believed that the use of this mercury-containing compound poses an unnecessary health risk to aquarium fish. Medications containing quinine are sold in pet shops, but most aquarists I have spoken with have had very inconsistent results with its use. In my opinion, the malachite/formalin treatment is the most effective, safest, rapid, and cost effective treatment for ich.

Slimy skin diseases, also known as blue slime diseases, are caused by a number of different externally parasitic protozoans that infect the skin and gills of aquarium fish. The most common belong to the genera *Ichthyobodo* (formerly *Costia*), *Chilodonella,* and *Trichodina.* It is most practical to discuss them as a group since they all produce similar symptoms and are treated in a similar fashion. Accurate identification is only possible with microscopic examination of a mucous smear taken from an infected fish.

In an attempt to flush the parasites from their body surface, infected fishes produce copious quantities of thick mucous. This is the cause of the slimy bluish appearance. The first symptoms often involve the fins or back, gradually spreading to other areas including the gills. The fish appears lethargic and may show labored breathing. In advanced cases, the fins and skin become reddened or ulcerated, and may slough in patches. The rapidity of the disease is dependent on the causative agent. Once the gills are involved, death comes swiftly.

Slime diseases are cured by adding two drops of formalin to each gallon (3.8 L) of water. (Formalin is a 37

Ich on a goldfish. This is the first fish disease most aquarists will encounter; fortunately, it is both easily recognized and treated.

percent by weight solution of formaldehyde in water.) This treatment should be repeated three times at three-day intervals. Improvement can be seen within 24 hours.

Caution: When using formaldehyde, always maintain good aeration and regularly check water quality. Do not breathe the vapors or get the chemical on your skin; Formaldehyde is a poison and classified as a potential carcinogen. No water changes are required between treatments since this chemical slowly dissipates from the water. The treatment is harmless to plants.

Care and Feeding of Piranhas

Basic Considerations

When kept under suitable conditions piranhas are hardy and adapt easily to aquarium life. Failures can usually be attributed to a lack of understanding of their needs and peculiarities, or notably poor husbandry techniques.

Unlike some South American freshwater fishes that are very demanding as to water quality and temperature, piranhas are easily satisfied. They do well in soft to moderately hard water and adapt to a pH range of at least 5.5 to 8.0. Water temperatures in the low 70s to the mid-80s°F (24–31°C) suit them very well. Of course, sudden changes in any of these parameters should be avoided.

It is common behavior for newly purchased piranhas to race for cover at

Piranhas are usually very shy and tend to hide when first introduced into your aquarium.

one's approach, spend much of the time hiding, and show a reluctance to emerge when fed. This nervousness is to be expected and will slowly diminish as they become secure with their surroundings and accustomed to the normal human activity around and within their aquarium. No attempts should ever be made to prod them into view or remove hiding places; this will only increase their stress levels and exacerbate their nervousness.

Mixing Piranha Species

The idea of having an aquarium devoted to a mixed group of piranhas is very tantalizing. Not much work has been done along these lines, but I would expect it to have a very limited chance of success. With the exception of the genus *Pygocentrus,* most adult piranhas feed heavily upon the fins of other fishes, including those of other piranhas. The more solitary species are known to attack others of their own kind. Even when only one species of the normally shoaling *Serrasalmus* is kept in a group, fin predation may become a problem. This can be minimized by keeping them in a very large aquarium with adequate cover where each individual is able to stake out a territory of its own or escape the aggressive actions of its tankmates. Even the larger *Serrasalmus* piranha species, which are mainly piscivorous as adults, are voracious fin predators when small. In my personal experiences it has been impossible to successfully keep more than one young

Serrasalmus piranha of any species per aquarium. Experimentally placing *Serrasalmus* species (red-throated, elongate, or black piranha), of any age with red-bellied piranhas has almost invariably resulted in severe damage to the fins and bodily integrity of the red-bellies. One notable exception is a mixed group of approximately 20 *S. spilopleura* and one *P. nattereri* that presently share a 500-gallon (185 L) reserve tank at the Dallas Aquarium.

If you should wish to keep a group of piranhas together I would recommend that you choose the commonly available red-bellied piranha or another of its genus. These three *Pygocentrus* species often live in large groups and under aquarium conditions tend to tolerate each others' company. Minor skirmishes resulting in injury should be expected, but normally these are not of a life-threatening nature. I have not been able to document any attempts at keeping more than one species of this genus together, but feel it would be worth trying. The biggest obstacle to this experiment would be obtaining the fish; the Orinoco red-bellied piranha is only rarely imported and I have never seen *P. piraya* on any wholesaler's list.

Mixing Piranhas with Other Species

The mixing of piranhas with other fish in the home aquarium is a subject of much controversy and interest. Possibly the most memorable piranha display I have ever seen is at the Dallas Aquarium in Dallas, Texas. Over 30 adult red-bellied piranhas share their 3,000-gallon (11,100 L) heavily planted and skylit aquarium with approximately 400 neon tetras, 100 marble hatchetfish, 200 bleeding heart tetras, and 200 gold tetras. These brightly colored, small schooling species are totally ignored as they swim in and among the shoal of piranhas. In addition to providing a multispecies "biotope" approach to the display of piranhas, it invariably amazes visitors with its beauty. At first thought such a mixed species group might seem impossible, but the reason for its success is quite simple: Piranhas are not adapted nor behaviorally programmed to feed upon prey items that are very small compared to their own size. With care, it is possible for the home aquarist with a large aquarium to duplicate a display of this type on a smaller scale. To be successful it is essential that only fish considerably smaller than the piranhas be used. These relative size differences are more easily accomplished if the piranhas are adults at least eight inches (18.3 cm), long with the small fish under one and three quarters inches (4.44 cm). Even large piranhas feed in nature upon fish as small as adult *Astyanax* species that average under four inches (9.1 cm) in total length. A small shoal of red-bellied piranhas or a single specimen of the larger nonsocial *Serrasalmus* species could be used in attempting to develop a mixed species piranha aquarium. I have successfully kept a single adult red-throated piranha with a small group of two-striped dwarf cichlid *(Apistogramma bitaeniata)* and a few immature splashing tetras (*Pyrrhulina sp.*) in a 50-gallon (190 L) aquarium. The dwarf cichlids even successfully reproduced and raised a group of young.

A totally different approach can be used when attempting to add other fish to an aquarium containing a *Pygocentrus* species. The red-bellied pacu is a mimic of the red-bellied piranhas. There are a number of reports of pacus being kept successfully with red-bellied piranhas of similar size. When I was employed at the Dallas Aquarium we experimentally placed two 12-inch (30.4 cm) pacus in a 500-gallon (1,900 L) reserve tank containing nine adult red-bellied piranhas.

This subadult Serrasalmus *of the* spilopleura *complex shows the results of severe fin predation by others of its own kind. After it was placed in a tank of its own, the fins quickly regenerated.*

This group lived amiably together for a number of months until the piranhas were transferred for display purposes. (The pacus were not used because we did not wish to have this herbivorous species consume the aquatic

An adult aquarium specimen of the fish commonly sold as red-throated, or diamond piranha, a member of the S. spilopleura *complex of species.*

vegetation in the display aquarium.) On numerous occasions, large plecostomus-type catfish species have been successfully kept with the red-bellied piranhas.

It is essential to the success of such mixed species piranha aquariums that the fish not be overcrowded. Crowding of piranhas would only encourage territorial aggression, which could be directed at the other species as well as each other. Overcrowding of aquariums also adversely affects water quality, making the fish more subject to illness and disease.

Diets in Captivity

In nature piranhas consume a widely varied diet; in captivity a similar regimen should be adhered to. Only by feeding a variety of nutritious foods can dietary difficiencies and impaired health be prevented.

The amount of food required to keep piranhas healthy varies with the age of the fish. When fed more than required, fish rapidly become overweight, a common condition that should be avoided. Obesity subjects a fish to a variety of health problems, including fatty livers, and shortens their potential life spans. I would recommend feeding adult piranhas no more than every other day. Young piranhas that are actively growing require proportionately more food than adult specimens and should be fed once daily as much as they will consume in four or five minutes.

The Danger of Using Live Foods

Sadly, there is a certain small segment of the aquarium hobby that seems to delight in watching piranhas and other predatory species attack and devour other live fish. Although piranhas only reluctantly learn to accept flake and pellet foods, the use of live feeder fish is definitely *not* needed to keep them healthy. More importantly, this practice poses a significant threat to the well-being of your fish. Feeder goldfish and minnows are host to a plethora of internal and external parasites and diseases that can be easily transmitted to your piranhas. Ich, flukes, anchor worms, and hexamita are just a few of the potentially serious problems that can be introduced into your aquarium with live feeder fish.

Newly acquired piranhas may at first appear reluctant to accept nonliving foods, but this is more an expression of their shyness, than of their feeding habits. Until the piranhas become accustomed to the presence of people, all that may be needed is for the aquarist to withdraw for a while after feeding the fish. In an hour or two, all uneaten food should be removed. In nature all piranhas are opportunistic scavengers, their excellent sense of smell making it easy for them to locate appropriate nonliving food items of both animal and vegetable nature.

If you feel that you must use live fish to feed your piranhas, they should first be put through a thorough quarantine period that includes treatment for flukes (see pages 53–54). This requires the inconvenience of permanently devoting a quarantine aquarium to feeder fish. Living foods that pose less of a hazard to the health of your fish are earthworms and live brine shrimp. Both are eagerly consumed by piranhas of appropriate size.

Suitable foods for piranhas include (clockwise from top) frozen whole small fishes, frozen krill, fresh or boiled beans and other vegetables, and strips of lean beef heart, fish, or shrimp flesh.

Frozen Foods

A varied assortment of frozen foods should be the basis of the piranha diet. The process of freezing destroys most, but not all, larger parasites and many protozoans. Unfortunately, organisms such as the causative agent of fish tuberculosis are not affected, but a well-balanced diet based upon frozen foods helps keep your fish in optimal health and thus increases their resistance to disease.

Whole bait minnows: Near the top of the list of recommended frozen food is frozen whole bait minnows. They supply the nutritional benefits of whole fish, while minimizing the chances of introducing dangerous pathogens into the aquarium. In addition to supplying needed protein they are also an excellent source of vitamins and minerals. They are stocked by most pet shops and bait supply houses, are easily stored, convenient to use, and readily recognized by your fish as a food item. Always thaw them before feeding.

Frozen krills: Other excellent foods are the frozen krills (*Euphasia superba* and *pacifica*). Not only do these small marine shrimps supply protein and needed trace elements, but their shells are a rich source of carotenes that help in the development of the attractive red and yellow colors found in many piranhas.

Other Recommended Foods

Strips of lean meat such as trimmed beef heart, and pieces of fish and shrimp sold for human consumption can help vary the diet of your piranhas. Many species of piranhas also readily accept vegetable foods. Knowing their feeding habits in nature, this should not be surprising. Cooked lima beans, peas, and string beans are some of the vegetables that I have found to be well accepted.

Commercial Diets

Pet shops offer many different brands of nutritionally complete frozen diets for aquarium fish that are incorporated within a gelatin base. The better brands have an excellent balance of both animal and vegetable ingredients. Piranhas quickly learn to accept them and they can be used as a major portion of their diet. It is also possible to make such a gel-based diet at home, but it is a bit messy. There is also the possibility that it will not be well balanced and include all necessary ingredients.

Processed Dry Foods

In this category are the multitude of flake, pelleted, and stick-shaped dry foods available. For the sake of this discussion freeze-dried foods are included in this category. Although many are nutritionally well balanced, piranhas do not generally accept these foods well but, with patience, it is possible to train some individuals to accept them. There is a better chance of success when you are working with very young fish. While convenient, dry foods should only be considered as a supplement and not the major component of any piranha diet.

Aquarium Maintenance

Careful observation and routine maintenance, while not very time consuming, are essential for the continued health and beauty of your aquarium.

A neglected aquarium soon becomes unsightly. Permitting aquarium conditions to deteriorate also predisposes your fish to illness and disease by lowering their resistance to infection.

The Aquarists' Tool Chest

Some basic equipment needed for routine maintenance are:
- chemicals to neutralize chlorine and chloramines in tap water
- spare airstones
- inexpensive test kits to measure pH and ammonia levels
- fish nets of various sizes
- a combination syphon hose and gravel washer
- algae scrubber pads

Depending upon the type of filter being used, replacement filtration material may also be needed.

It is a prudent measure to also have on hand a basic emergency supply kit. When an essential piece of equipment breaks down, it is often impossible to quickly buy a replacement. At the minimum this should include an extra aquarium heater, a replacement air pump or pump repair kit, and a spare thermometer. These items require only a modest expenditure, but can make the difference between life and death of your aquarium's inhabitants.

Daily Care

At least once daily the aquarium should be given a careful visual once-over. This is conveniently performed at feeding time. All fish should be examined for signs of disease or injury. If either are found, appropriate action should be quickly initiated. Any uneaten pieces of food that remain from a previous feeding should be promptly removed to avoid fouling the water. If you feed your fish a proper amount, and they are healthy, there should not be any leftover food in the first place.

Water temperature: Check the water temperature for any unexplained change. This could indicate that the heater's temperature setting has somehow been tampered with, or it could be the sign of a faulty heater. Thermostats may stick and heating elements eventually burn out. Do not assume that just because the heater's indictor light is on that it is working properly. The pilot light often remains permanently lit when the heating element is burned out, and the aquarium's water temperature drops below the thermostat's setting. Water droplets condensing on the inside surface of the heater's glass tube indicate a leak that can result in a short circuit. Immediately replace all faulty heaters with a new one.

Airstones and filtration systems: Check all airstones and air-driven filtration systems regularly to be certain that they are working properly. Decreased air flow may be caused by clogged airstones or leaky pump diaphragms. All airstones eventually clog from a buildup of minerals, bacteria, and dust particles. To check if they are clogged, remove them from the air line and blow through them. If you experience excessive resistance, promptly replace the airstone. If this does not rectify the situation it could be due to a fault in the pump. This can be checked by replacing the pump with one of a similar type. If this solves the problem the diaphragm probably requires replacing. Repair kits are available for most brands of pumps at your pet store. At these times the usefulness of a spare air pump becomes obvious.

Algae

Algae buildup on the glass walls of the aquarium requires periodic attention. Although these microscopic plants are not harmful, they are unsightly and impair the ability to visually check the health and behavior of the fish. The common practice of

Magnetic algae cleaners are most useful in aquariums that do not have overly thick glass.

retarding algae buildup by adding a species of algae-eating catfish to the aquarium is not practical in a tank containing piranhas. Although red-bellied piranhas often ignore the catfish (particularly if the catfish is fairly large), most other species would consider them just another meal. There are many different brands of algae cleaning pads available. I recommend the magnetic types or those with an attached handle. These permit the cleaning of the glass without placing one's hands in with the piranhas. Because of piranhas' sensitivity to many chemicals, I would avoid the general use of algacidal chemicals without prior thorough testing.

Water Changes

One of the most misunderstood procedures in aquarium care is the need for frequent partial water changes. This is *not* the same thing as adding water to make up for evaporation. When water evaporates, the minerals stay behind. If you only replace what has evaporated you would be gradually increasing the hardness of your

An algae cleaning pad permanently mounted on a long handle allows you to clean the aquarium's glass without placing your hands inside the tank.

The regular use of a gravel washer ensures the proper functioning of undergravel filters.

aquarium's water. No matter how efficient the filtration, or how well you care for your aquarium, a slow buildup of harmful organic chemicals and minerals in the water from the byproducts of fish and plant metabolism will also be produced. Periodic partial water changes is a way of preventing this. Generally, a 15–20 percent water change weekly is recommended. This should be combined with the syphoning of built-up debris from the substrate. Be certain that the water you add is the same temperature as that in the aquarium and don't forget to use the chloramine remover!

Care of Filters

Filters of all types require regular maintenance to perform at an optimal level, the servicing needed depending upon the type of filter in use. Since virtually all filters eventually develop important biological activity (see Biologic Filtration, page 37), it is a good idea not to clean the entire filter system of an aquarium at one time.

Undergravel filters have a tendency to pack and clog with debris. This lessens their efficiency by reducing the water flow through the gravel bed. How rapidly this occurs depends on many factors such as the number of fish, the amount being fed, and the depth and particle size of the gravel. Care of undergravel filters involves occasionally stirring the surface of the gravel to prevent packing, and the less frequent removal of excess organic debris from within the gravel bed with the use of a gravel washer. Gravel washers are nothing more than a syphon hose attached to a section of rigid plastic tube that is about three times greater in diameter than the syphon. These washers permit the aquarist to clean excess debris from within the gravel without removing the gravel from the aquarium. When using a gravel washer, try to avoid excessive

A group of adult red-bellied piranhas sharing their large display aquarium with neon tetras.

disturbance to the roots of live aquarium plants.

Box, canister, and power filters all utilize some type of filter pad or floss to trap suspended matter. As this clogs, the ability of the water to pass through it is impaired and the filter media should be cleaned or replaced. You will quickly learn how frequently your filter requires such care. Over time, activated carbon loses its ability to serve as a chemical filtering medium. Not only does it lose its power of adsorption, but its pores become clogged with bacteria and foreign matter. Aquarium water often develops a slight yellow tinge when the carbon has lost its activity. This is an indication that it is time to replace the carbon in your filter.

If you are using power filters, it is a good idea to clean the impeller of the motor while changing the filtering medium. A buildup of slime or foreign matter on the impeller reduces the flow rate and strains the motor. Instructions for this procedure are supplied with the filter.

Trickle or wet/dry filters require the least amount of maintenance. Other than following the recommended servicing procedures for their water pump, and checking that the water in the sump is at the proper level, all that is required is the cleaning or replacement of the prefilter material as needed.

Safety Precautions

The aquarist should never ignore the potential danger of receiving a severe piranha bite. Feeding your piranhas and servicing your piranha aquarium should always be performed in a way that will minimize such chances. Most aquarium fishes—piranhas included—quickly become conditioned to feeding times and procedures. Anticipating a meal, they rush to the surface as soon as they see a

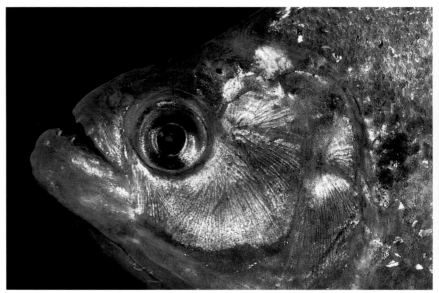

The teeth of living piranhas are almost totally hidden by the lips. This is an adult red-throated, or diamond piranha (S. spilopleura complex) from the Rio Napo, Peru.

When netting piranhas, use a large enough net and catch them one at a time.

piece of food or other object enter the aquarium, even the aquarist's fingertips! The potential for injury occurs at a time when a piranha accidentally confuses the aquarist's hand with a piece of food. These accidents usually happen the moment the fingertips just break the surface of the water, and not once the entire hand is submerged. They can easily result in the amputation of a fingertip and considerable loss of blood. If you must place your hands in a tank containing piranhas, do it in a way that minimizes the chances of the fish "thinking" it is food. Feeding them first is one way of reducing their feeding response.

Piranhas are not by nature aggressive to their human caretakers. At public aquariums an aquarist may regularly be required to enter the large piranha displays for servicing. At these times the piranhas demonstrate their inherent shyness by retreating to the far corners of the exhibit.

Always keep your hands away from the net when transferring a piranha to another aquarium. Use a net that is deep enough to keep the piranha from jumping out, and complete the transfer before the piranha can bite through the net and fall to the floor. A frightened piranha flopping on the floor snaps defensively at any object that approaches it and their agility and speed can be quite surprising. Such a fall can also severely injure the fish. For safety reasons, I prefer to quickly transfer the netted piranha to a bucket containing water from their aquarium, and moving it in this container.

pH

Many aquarists are taught to be overly concerned about pH. Piranhas do very well within a range of at least 6.5–7.5. Slight fluctuations within this acceptable limit are normal and nothing to worry about, but sudden or drastic changes are another matter. Any deliberate changes in the pH of your aquarium should be done slowly. The major cause of pH instability in an established aquarium is poor husbandry techniques. A severe drop in pH into the excessively acidic zone is more common than a rise. It is most commonly caused by pollution of the water due to the excessive buildup of decomposing organic matter. This can be the presence of uneaten food, dead fish, or filter inefficiency. The inadvertent use of rocks containing limestone, excessive aeration, or an overabundance of live plants will cause the pH to rise. Due to its lack of buffering calcium salts, very soft water reacts more quickly to these factors than water of greater hardness.

It is wise to check the pH of an established aquarium's water once weekly, more frequently if it is newly set up or if your water is very soft. Needed short-term adjustments can be made with partial water changes or the use of chemicals available at your pet shop that are specifically formulated to raise or lower the pH. To permanently solve the problem involves analyzing your husbandry techniques and making the necessary changes.

Breeding Piranhas

Breeding in Captivity

Only three or four species of piranhas have been bred in captivity. Almost all of these have occurred at public aquariums where a single-species shoal of adult specimens were housed in aquariums of at least 1,000 gallons (3,800 L). With few exceptions, a nest was constructed among rooted vegetation and one or both members of the pair protected the spawn. It is not known whether all piranhas, especially those belonging to the less evolved genera of *Pygopristis, Pristobrycon,* and *Catoprion* practice similar forms of reproduction. Hopefully, dedicated home aquarists will eventually provide answers to these and many other questions that have so far eluded researchers.

Piranhas are not sexually dimorphic, meaning males and females are similar in appearance. To the practiced eye females filled with spawn appear heavier than males, and in a few species males in breeding condition may possibly become darker in color than the females.

I would recommend that a novice at piranha breeding start with *S. naterreri,* the red-bellied piranha. This is a very attractive and hardy species, easily identified at all sizes by body shape and markings, and the most frequently imported. Because of its schooling nature, it is also one of the easiest piranhas to keep in a group. It is not surprising that the red-bellied piranha has been bred in captivity more frequently than any other species.

Necessary Commitments

You should realize that attempting to breed piranhas will involve considerable commitments of time, money, and room. A shoal of six to eight breeding size piranhas will require an aquarium of at least 100 to 250 gallons (380–950 L) capacity. To avoid serious fighting and cannibalism, the more solitary fin- and scale-eating species require more room per fish than those that in nature live in small shoals or schools. Not only is an aquarium of this size quite expensive, but it takes up a lot of room and is exceedingly heavy. The floors of most homes are not built to support such a massive concentration of weight.

Where to Find
the Breeding Piranhas

Don't expect to find a school of breeding-size piranhas at your local pet shop—adult piranhas are rarely exported from South America. Because of their large size and need for individual bagging, the cost of shipping them is prohibitively high. There is also the probability of them biting through their plastic shipping bags and arriving dead. This is why we invariably see small piranhas for sale.

I would advise the potential piranha breeder to purchase a group of young fish and grow them to maturity, which, even with good care will take about two years. Always buy a few more fish than you will need when they reach adulthood, as there will almost always be some losses due to aggression and cannibalism or disease. A factor often complicating the selection of young fishes to buy is that they are sometimes imported in mixed species lots. Young *Serrasalmus* piranhas are often offered for sale as white piranhas, a name with no scientific standing that is applied to numerous species. Immature—and even adult—of many *Serrasalmus* piranhas are very difficult to tell apart, and may dramatically change in color and shape as they grow. This can conceivably result in the aquarist ending up with an incompatible school of more than one species. By now you can begin to see why very few aquarists have attempted to breed piranhas.

The Use of Plants

Even with a group of mature piranhas, getting them to reproduce involves both skill and a degree of luck. All reports indicate that piranhas like to construct their nests within thickets of submerged aquatic plants or fine roots. You should therefore thickly plant a portion of the aquarium with groves of plants such as the various V*allisneria, Sagittaria, Bacopa,* or *Hygrophila* species. Bunches of unrooted plants or coconut fiber weighted down with small rocks have also proved successful.

Studying the Seasons

We can learn a lot from studying piranhas' natural biology. In nature they breed at the beginning of the rainy season. During the dry season most of the rivers and streams slow their flow, and increase in temperature. Dissolved oxygen levels often drop significantly due to the combination of the lack of water movement, warmer water temperatures, and the breakdown of organic matter. In isolated lakes food often becomes scarce.

With the onset of the rainy season, the frequent showers cause a slight cooling of the water, dilute the noxious organics, and decrease the hardness

levels. As a result of increased water movement and the splashing action of the raindrops, dissolved oxygen levels return to normal levels. As the waters rise, the fishes are able to travel to areas that have a greater abundance of food, and they rapidly improve in condition. Attempting to partially simulate these conditions in your aquarium may increase your chances of encouraging your piranhas to spawn.

To simulate the dry season I would suggest that you reduce the amount and frequency of feedings and raise the water temperature to the mid-80s°F (30°C). You can also reduce the frequency and volume of water changes, always being careful not to endanger the health of your fishes. After a couple of months the filtration and aeration should be increased, and frequent partial water changes initiated. The setting on your heater can be lowered to the mid- to upper 70s°F (25°C) and the amount and variety of foods offered should be increased. Hopefully, this simulation of the beginning of the rainy season will induce your piranhas to start planning a family. Water hardness and pH does not seem to be critical as long as you stay away from the extremes. Piranhas have been bred in soft to moderately hard water that varied in pH from slightly acidic to quite alkaline.

Courtship

An early sign of courtship is a male starting to chase and pursue the females. Displays by one or both fish may take the form of body wagging, darkening of color, and a pair swimming in tight head-to-tail circles. Pairing and courtship can be rather rough, with both individuals suffering minor wounds, split fins, and missing scales. As the pair bond develops, the two fishes will start to defend a specific territory. Any other member of the school that approaches this area is attacked and driven off, often resulting in severe injuries and even death to the trespasser. The larger the tank, the easier it is for the other fishes to keep their distance.

Piranha Fry

When piranha fry become free-swimming, they are large enough to consume live, newly-hatched, brine shrimp. You can purchase brine shrimp eggs at your pet shop. They are easily hatched—just follow the instructions on the container. With frequent feedings baby piranhas grow rapidly. Piranha fry are very sensitive to poor water conditions and elevated ammonia and nitrite levels. A major factor that contributes to these harmful conditions is the decomposition of uneaten food. Brine shrimp do not survive long in freshwater; therefore, it is essential that all dead shrimp be syphoned from the tank daily before they can foul the water. A small number of pond or ramshorn snails added to the aquarium will also help eliminate the dead shrimp.

As the babies grow, other food items should be added to their diet. Commercially available frozen fish foods using gelatin as a binder, frozen small krill (Euphasia pacifica), fish flesh, lean meat, and shrimp are all eagerly consumed. It is important to realize that very small piranhas do not have the razor-sharp teeth and powerful jaws of larger specimens. They are unable to sever mouthfuls of food from a large food item, and all meat and fish offered to them should be finely ground; a food processor performs this duty beautifully. Small piranhas can be easily trained to accept a good brand of flake food. Continue to be vigilant about removing any uneaten food and performing frequent partial water changes. As your fishes grow they will require progressively more space. A commonly noticed problem when young piranhas are kept under crowded conditions is serious fin predation and rampant cannibalism. This is not surprising knowing their feeding habits in nature.

Rate of Growth

Piranhas raised under good conditions grow rapidly. At the Shedd Aquarium, red-throated piranha fry attained lengths of approximately three quarters of an inch (1.90 cm) in six weeks, while red-bellied piranhas grew to five inches (12.7 cm) in eight months. These measurements are consistent with those documented to be attained in nature. Maturity for these two species is probably reached in two years.

Disposing of Surplus Piranhas

Reasons for Disposal

The disposal of unwanted aquarium fish is an important subject that has not been given the attention it deserves. It is essential that surplus aquarium fishes be disposed of in a responsible way. For various reasons, the time may come when you wish to part with some or all of your piranhas. You may be moving to a state that bans the possession of piranhas. Poor planning combined with impulse buying often results in piranhas quickly outgrowing or overcrowding their aquarium. You may also find that with time your taste in aquarium fish has changed. Perhaps your skill in aquarium husbandry has resulted in the successful spawning of your piranhas. Piranha spawns are very large, often numbering in the thousands, and in a home aquarium it would be impossible to raise all the fry resulting from a large hatch. The time to develop plans for the disposal of your young piranhas is *before* you attempt to breed them.

Options

There are few options available to one wishing to dispose of surplus or unwanted fishes. One is indeed fortunate to find a friend or fellow aquarium society member who would gladly accept them. Many hobbyists are under the mistaken assumption that pet shops or public aquariums gladly accept all donations, but these facilities should not be thought of as dumping grounds for unwanted fishes.

Aquarium stores are in the business of selling fish and will only accept those species that are popular and in demand. Piranhas have a rather limited appeal, and are usually stocked in small numbers. It is difficult for the average person to fully comprehend the volume of calls received by public aquariums from people wishing to donate unwanted fishes. Although pacus, oscars, and large pimelodid catfish top this list, piranhas are not far behind. Usually, the donors also make it clear that they wish to have visiting privileges and want their fish to be displayed for all to see! In addition to their space limitations, these institutions carefully develop master plans relating to their fish collection. With few exceptions they will only accept donations of specimens that are needed and consistent with their mission.

Environmental Consequences of Irresponsible Disposal

When faced with the reality that the world is not anxiously awaiting the donation of their previously cherished pet fishes, many people think that releasing them into local waters is a kindly alternative or a quick solution to their problem. Regardless of motive, this is among the most environmentally and morally irresponsible actions that a tropical fish hobbyist can perform. The ever more frequent capture of released tropical fishes in local waters is a major cause of the increasingly restrictive state and local legislation affecting our hobby.

Never *release any aquarium fishes, including piranhas, into waters where they are not native.*

In most portions of the United States climatic and environmental factors preclude the survival of these foreign species. Instead of doing your fishes a favor, you are sentencing them to a lingering death. Of more importance is the threat of severe and unpredictable environmental consequences.

Exotics directly compete with native species for the available space and food resources. Even seemingly innocuous species may prove devastating to the native fauna. For instance, the mosquito fish, *Gambusia affinis,* has been deliberately introduced for mosquito control into portions of the United States and foreign countries where it is not native. Who would have predicted the serious effects this competitive small livebearer would have on the native fish faunas? In many desert springs of our own country this species is now one of the major threats to the survival of the endemic fish populations!

The release of a species into an area where it is not native also poses the risk of introducing a potentially

devastating exotic disease or parasite. There are many such documented cases, including the establishment of an Asian tapeworm into populations of endangered fish species in the western United States.

Predatory exotic species can be particularly catastrophic. Most of us have heard of the tragic effects the introduction of Nile Perch (*Lates* sp.) had upon the unique fish fauna of Africa's Lake Victoria. The second largest lake in the world, Victoria was home to over 400 species of fishes found nowhere else. The Nile perch has eaten its way through this lake. The result has been mass extinctions of a majority of the native species and a devastating effect upon both the lake's ecology and the native peoples of the area. It is almost superfluous to explain that it is a technical impossibility to remove the Nile perch from this enormous lake, 26,000 square miles (68,000 square kilometers) in area.

Exotic species can also affect the ecology of an area by altering the environment. As an example, the bottom-grubbing feeding behavior of introduced European carp and goldfish results in increased turbidity and limited visibility for sight-feeding species. The suspended silt may also suffocate the eggs of native fish species.

Social and Legal Factors

The capture of most species of released aquarium fish in a local lake may arouse feelings of curiosity or indignation, but when this fish is a piranha there is the fear factor to contend with. All the local news media carry the story and there are outcries from well-meaning extremists to ban the import of all tropical fishes as a public safety concern. This is definitely not the type of publicity the aquarium hobby needs.

Lastly, the release of fishes into waters where they are not native is illegal and can result in severe penalties for the offender.

Euthanasia

With all that in mind, what are aquarists to do when they cannot find other homes for fishes they must dispose of? Very often, other than rethinking the situation and keeping the fish, the solution of choice is euthanasia. I fully realize that no feeling person enjoys having to put a pet to "sleep," but at times it is the best and kindest choice. This procedure can also be used to end the suffering of a terminally ill or injured piranha.

Many techniques of euthanasia have been advocated for fish. The majority of people would say that the most important criteria to be considered are that the procedure does not cause pain and suffering to the fish and that it is foolproof. My technique of choice is to place the fish in a small aquarium or container of water to which is added an overdose of any commercially available fish tranquilizer or anesthetic. These can be obtained from pet shops and aquaculture supply houses. Once the fish is fully sedated and nonreactive to the touch, it can be transferred to a plastic bag or other receptacle with a small amount of the tranquilizer-containing water, and placed in a freezer until frozen. This technique avoids the unpleasant messiness of some other methods and creates minimal stress for the fish.

A Representative Cross-section of Piranha Species

The present state of piranha taxonomy makes it impossible to compile anything close to a complete, properly identified, photographic survey of this group of fishes. This chapter attempts to present to the reader a representative cross-section of these fascinating and diverse fishes. Both newly described and well-known species are represented. Every effort has been made to properly identify all fishes pictured. When a fish has commonly been known in the literature under other scientific names, these are placed in parenthesis. Where it is known, collection data is included in the photo captions. Many species of piranha do not yet have English common names, and others are referred to by more than one appellation. I have attempted to include common names used in the aquarium literature.

A short discussion is included for all species presented. Notes are included pertaining to ranges, habits, sizes at maturity, and diets in nature, as they are presently understood. Sizes are given in standard length—the distance from the tip of the snout to the base of the tail. All this information should only be taken as a very general guide. I expect much of it to be greatly expanded upon and modified by future research findings.

Genus *Pygocentrus*

Pygocentrus nattereri (P. stigmaterythraeus, Serrasalmus nattereri, Rooseveltiella nattereri, Serrasalmo piranha)

Common name: Red-bellied Piranha

Range: A huge area of Amazonia including the Peruvian and Brazilian Amazon, most of the major tributaries, and south to include the Rio Paraná and Paraguay. It is absent from the Orinoco and Guiana drainages.

Adult size: Approximately 12 inches (30.5 cm) standard length

Comments: This piranha is found most abundantly in whitewater habitats. It often travels in large, loosely organized groups that lack the precise organization seen in a true schooling fish. This species, and its two other *Pygocentrus* relatives, are the most

Young adult red-bellied piranha with spots that are mostly faded.

A three-month-old red-bellied piranha beginning to develop its red pigmentation.

Adult Orinoco red-bellied piranha. The black marking behind the gill is typical of this species, but lacking in P. nattereri.

carnivorous piranhas. A robust and powerful species, feeding voraciously upon fish flesh and whole fish, it will also attack and consume birds, mammals, and reptiles when such opportunities present themselves.

This best-known, wide-ranging, and beautifully colored species is the most frequently imported piranha, and one of the few that can be safely kept in groups. It is also the species most frequently bred in captivity. Young are heavily spotted with black. The red underside begins to develop at a very early age. As maturity is approached, the black spots fade and numerous spangles of gold and silver develop on their sides. Adults in full color almost give the appearance of having been dusted with glitter.

The three *Pygocentrus* species are largely responsible for the savage, man-eating reputation of piranhas. As we have seen, this perception is undeserved.

Pygocentrus cariba (Pygocentrus notatus, P. caribe, Serrasalmus notatus, S. nattereri, Taddyella notatus)

Common names: Orinoco red-bellied piranha, black-eared piranha, red-bellied piranha, capaburro

Range: Orinoco River drainage of Venezuela

Adult size: Approximately 12 inches (30.5 cm)

Comments: This species is the Orinoco equivalent of the Amazonian *P. nattereri*. As far as is known, the habits and diets of these two closely

A fisherman's catch of P. cariba *in breeding color. The red is almost totally obscured by the development of the black pigmentation. Llanos region, Venezuela.*

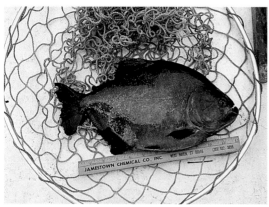

Adult black piranha caught on hook and line. Note the wire leader! Rio Branco, Brazil.

Young adult black piranha. This fish has not yet developed the dark body color, but clearly shows the red eye typical of the species. Peruvian Amazon near Nauta.

related species are very similar. Both have been known to attack the udders and genitals of wading cattle. Their extremely powerful jaws demand that they be treated with respect. When in breeding condition, Orinoco red-bellied piranhas turn almost uniformly black. Photographs of sexually active specimens have often been erroneously labeled as *S. niger,* a name with questionable taxonomic standing.

Juvenile S. rhombeus *four inches (10.2 mm) long. This is the stage at which they are often called white piranhas. Junction of Rio Napo with the Rio Tacshacuraray, Peru.*

The black shoulder spot is present in all but the smallest specimens.

This species has been much confused with *P. nattereri* both in the popular and scientific literature. Illustrations of it are often identified as *P. (Serrasalmus) nattereri,* and the range of the latter species is often incorrectly stated to include the Orinoco River.

Genus *Serrasalmus*

Serrasalmus rhombeus (*S. niger*)

Common names: Black piranha, white piranha, red-eyed piranha

Size: One of the largest piranhas, reaching a length of at least 18 inches (45.7 cm) and a weight in excess of five pounds (2.2 kg)

Range: Abundant within the entire Amazon and Orinoco River Basins and the rivers of the Guianas

Comments: This is a very abundant, widespread, and variable species that is often found in small, loosely organized shoals. Further taxonomic studies may possibly determine that what we refer to as the black piranha is in reality a complex of several closely related species.

The appearance of this species changes greatly with age. Young specimens five inches (12.7 cm) and smaller are basically diamond-shaped, silvery fish with numerous small dark spots. The tail has a terminal dark band and basal area. There may be a slight red or pinkish wash to the opercular region and the anal fin. At this stage they are often referred to as white piranhas. With maturity they become more massive, and deeper bodied. All colors progressively darken and the eyes become a distinctive ruby red.

Large adults are commonly a solid charcoal gray with iridescent purple and gold highlights. Due to the overall dark tone of the fins, the black tail edging may be difficult to perceive. This adult coloration is responsible for their common names of black piranha and red-eyed piranha. As is the case with Orinoco red-bellied piranhas in spawning condition, darkly colored large adult *S. rhombeus* are also frequently misidentified as *S. niger.*

When young, this species feeds heavily upon the fins of other fish. With increasing size their diet shifts to fish flesh and whole fish. Although a large and very powerful species, the black piranha has never been known to be dangerous to humans or larger warm-blooded prey. An adult black piranha in full color makes a very impressive display fish for the home or public aquarium.

Serrasalmus gouldingi

Common name: Goulding's Piranha

Range: Only known from the black-waters of the Negro, Casiquiare, Japurá, and Pacimoni rivers of Brazil and Venezuela

Size: A moderately large piranha, reaching a standard length of a little over 11 inches (28 cm).

Comments: This species was first described in 1992 by Fink and Machado-Allison, and named for Dr. Michael Goulding, the respected

Adult Goulding's piranha. The pale-colored eye, pattern of body spotting and clear edge to the tail separate it from its relative, the black piranha, which shares its range. Rio Negro near Barcellos, Brazil.

naturalist and writer whose research is contributing so much to our understanding of the Amazon region. Goulding's piranha superficially resembles the black piranha, which shares its range. Both are darkly colored as adult, but the eyes of Goulding's piranha are silvery blue to pale amber, and never red as in *S. rhombeus.* All

Juvenile Goulding's piranha. The vertically elongated body spots are already evident. Rio Negro near Barcellos, Brazil.

Manuel's piranha, Serrasalmus manueli, *can grow to at least two feet (61 cm) in length. Low Llanos region of Venezuela.*

unpaired fins of *S. gouldingi* are very darkly pigmented, the tail with a transparent, instead of black, terminal border. Characteristic of this species are faint, vertically elongated spots on the sides. Adults in breeding condition turn very dark with a purple luster, the body spots not being visible. Virtually nothing is known about their habits.

A young specimen of Manuel's piranha; it will become deeper bodied with maturity.

Serrasalmus manueli (Pygocentrus manueli)

Common name: Manuel's piranha

Range: Not clearly understood. Abundant in the Orinoco drainage where at many locales it is the most abundant piranha. This, or a very similar species, is also found in rivers of the lower Amazon region.

Size of adults: A large and rather massive piranha. Specimens from the Orinoco basin can exceed a standard length of 13 inches (33 cm); the form from the lower Amazon is reported to grow significantly larger.

Comments: This is a very distinctive fish with its prominent black shoulder bar and vertically elongated dark body markings. The throat and breast region often show considerable orange, and the tail invariably has a black basal region. Old adults may darken considerably. As with many piranhas, young specimens are more elongated and have more pointy snouts.

The habits of Manuel's piranhas are not well known. Limited studies have indicated that the bulk of its diet is comprised of fish and fish flesh, with a significant amount of plant matter sometimes being consumed. Although virtually unknown in the aquarium trade, this may soon change as shipments of tropical fish from Venezuela increase. It is a very attractive species that should definitely be looked for by piranha fanciers.

Serrasalmus spilopleura

Common names: Red-throated piranha, diamond piranha

Range: Widespread throughout the Amazon River and its tributaries, and the Rio Paraná and Paraguay systems

Adult size: A moderate-size piranha, adults averaging seven to eight inches (17.8–20 cm) in length

Comments: Present-day authorities feel that the fish we call *S. spilopleura* is probably a complex of closely related species. This may help explain the great variation in its appearance throughout its extensive range. Typical forms from the lower Amazon have a conspicuous subterminal black tail band, the very edge of this fin being transparent. Fish from the upper Amazon Basin in Peru, presently referred to as this species, may lack the hyaline tail border, the black edging to this fin being terminal. This is the form most commonly imported into the United States but they may eventually turn out to not be *S. spilopleura!* Medine's piranha *(S. medinei)* is a closely related species from Venezuela.

Young are typically pointy-snouted and long-jawed, their bodies marked by numerous black spots. With maturity they become deeper bodied and considerably more short-faced. Red or yellow pigment may develop on the throat, gill plate, and anal fin. In many populations the dark spotting becomes progressively more faint as they approach maturity. Breeding adults darken considerably, their sides becoming adorned with numerous spangles of silver or light blue. They are primarily fin feeders at all ages, with adults also consuming small fish and fish flesh.

This is one of the more commonly available piranha species. They are often present in shipments from Peru and Colombia. Because of their fin-eating tendencies, specimens available in pet shops are often badly mutilated. Young should be kept one per tank to avoid disfigurement and cannibalism. Public aquariums have had reasonable success keeping adult red-throated piranhas in larger groups, but their fins invariably show missing sections. This is one of the few piranhas that have been bred in captivity. Many forms of this fish are very attractive and worth keeping, but in the confines of an aquarium, they are often exceedingly shy and retiring.

A piranha of the Serrasalmus spilopleura *complex from the Peruvian Amazon. Rio Orosa.*

Serrasalmus irritans
Common name: None
Range: Savanna areas of Orinoco drainage; Venezuela
Adult size: A moderately small piranha, averaging no more than seven inches (17.5 cm) in length
Comments: This is an elongated and rather pointy-snouted species.

Subadult specimen of S. spilopleura *from the middle Amazon. Rio Purus, Brazil. Note the transparent edging of the tail.*

Adult Serrasalmus irritans *from Caño Maraca, Venezuela. This species maintains the fin- and scale-eating habits through adulthood.*

The upper half of its body is marked with numerous, relatively small dark spots and the tail displays a black basal area. The anal fin is almost entirely reddish. The diet of subadults *S. irritans* is composed primarily of fish fins. The stomach contents of larger specimens is a mixture of fish flesh, fins, scales, and entire small fish. In the popular aquarium literature, photos of this species have often been misidentified as *S. eigenmanni*, a rather similar species commonly found in the upper Orinoco of Venezuela.

As far as I can ascertain, this species is rarely imported for the aquarium trade; piranha fanatics should look for it in Venezuelan imports. Judging from what we know about this fish, its feeding habits would dictate that it must be kept by itself.

Serrasalmus elongatus (S. pingke)

Common name: Elongate Piranha

Range: Peruvian and Brazilian Amazon, Venezuela, and the Guianas

Adult size: A smaller species of piranha, rarely exceeding seven inches (17.5 cm) in standard length

Comments: This is the most elongated and least deep-bodied piranha species known. Most often an unmarked silver in color, specimens from Venezuela may have considerable red pigmentation on the gill cover and breast. Fins are most commonly hyaline, except for the tail, which may be diffusely dusky.

The elongate piranha is fast swimming, active, and solitary. Its long jaws are perfectly adapted to removing scales and pieces of fins from its prey species. The hunting strategy of the elongate piranha appears to be a combination of ambush and swift attacks. It is often found in areas with more current than are other piranhas. I have collected it at the mouths of rather swiftly flowing streams, where it was most probably lying in wait for unsuspecting prey to be washed its way.

Due to its solitary nature, general lack of any bright colors, and aggressiveness, the elongate piranha is rarely imported. This is unfortunate because it is a most interesting fish that, in my experience, lacks much of the shyness so common to most piranhas in captivity. Obviously, it must be kept by itself, as it will readily attack

Serrasalmus elongatus *is the most slender of all known piranha species. The saw-tooth ventral keel typical of all serrasalmines is very well developed.* Rio Orosa, Peru.

and destroy the fins and skin of any other fish, including others of its own kind. It will also chase down and devour fish that are small enough to be swallowed whole.

Genus *Pristobrycon*
Pristobrycon maculipinnis
Common Name: Locally called *piranha colorado,* which translates into red piranha

Range: Known only from one black-water tributary of the Brazo Casiquiare and another of the Atabapo River, both in southern Venezuela

Adult size: A large *Pristobrycon,* attaining a standard length of at least nine and three quarters inches (24.5 cm)

Comments: This is a strikingly beautiful, recently described (1992), and apparently locally distributed species. The heavily marbled body is dark olive above, shading into rich orange-gold sides. This color is a more intense orange ventrally, and extends into the lower fins. The heavy black speckling of all unpaired fins is responsible for its scientific name (*maculipinnis* = spotted fins). When in spawning condition, all colors deepen and intensify, with blue and purple highlights appearing on the body.

The diet of this fish is typical of pira-nhas belonging to this genus, being comprised mainly of finely masticated seeds with a smaller percentage of other plant material, invertebrates, and scales. These dietary findings corre-late well with its unusually long intes-tine (for a piranha).

Unfortunately, this fish is yet to be imported. It would undoubtedly make a wonderful display fish for either the home aquarium or public institutions.

Pristobrycon striolatus (Pygocentrus striolatus, Serrasalmus striolatus, Pygopristis antoni)
Common name: Black-tailed piranha

Pristobrycon maculipinnis *is a large and beautifully colored piranha. Rio Pasimoni, Upper Orinoco drainage, Venezuela.*

Range: Virtually all of the Amazon and Orinoco Basins, and the Guianas; they have been collected from both white and blackwater habitats.

Adult size: This is a medium-size piranha, averaging less than eight inches (20 cm) in standard length

Comments: So round and laterally compressed are adults of this species

A very nicely colored specimen of the black-tailed piranha, Pristobrycon striolatus. *Caño Caicara, Venezuela.*

that the casual observer can almost confuse it with a silver dollar (Genus *Metynnis*); however, its typical piranha dentition, consisting of a single row of interlocking triangular teeth, is all that is needed for proper taxonomic placement. The disk-like body is silver and sprinkled with small dark specks. Considerable red-orange is usually present on the operculum, lower breast area, and anal fin of adults. The basal area of the tail is conspicuously black. Juveniles are more diamond-shaped, with a variable amount of red in the anal fin. The black area of the tail is also less extensive.

Adults and subadults of this weak-jawed piranha subsist mainly on a diet of seeds. As is common to all piranhas, very small specimens consume aquatic insects and fish fins. This wide-ranging species is sporadically imported in small numbers. Having had very limited experience caring for the black-tailed piranha, I cannot say whether or not adult specimens can be kept in groups without undesirable consequences. Juveniles will definitely attack the fins of any tankmates—including members of their own species—and must be housed singly.

Adult five-cusped piranha. This is the only species within the genus Pygopristis.

Genus *Pygopristis*
Pygopristis denticulatus
(Serrasalmus denticulatus, Pygopristis punctatus, P. fumarius)

Common name: Five-cusped piranha, big-toothed piranha (this name, which is sometimes used in aquarium literature, is inappropriate; its teeth are not unusually large, but in fact are proportionately smaller than those of many other piranhas)

Range: Not clearly understood; definitely found in the Lower Amazon, Rio Negro, and Rio Orinoco drainages; probably also present in the Peruvian Amazon and Guianan drainage

Adult size: Similar in size to the black-tailed piranha, rarely exceeding eight inches (20 cm) in standard length

Comments: Resembling *Pristobrycon striolatus* in size and shape, this sole member of its genus is the only piranha with five-cusped teeth. It appears to prefer heavily vegetated clear and blackwater habitats. Generally found at low population densities, we once collected numerous specimens in a blackwater lake off the Rio Dimini (a tributary of the Rio Negro) during a cardinal tetra field survey with Dr. Labbish N. Chao of the Universidad do Amazonas, Manaus, Brazil.

The five-cusped piranha is usually a silvery fish with quite a bit of red-orange on the operculum, lower sides, and much of the fins. A large dark spot is usually present on the gill plate, and the basal half of the tail is black. There is a series of irregular, fine, and indistinct dusky bars crossing the flanks. At times, very dark specimens of this fish are captured. These show very little orange color, being a deep olive-brown in tone with dark basal areas to all fins except the pectorals (see photo page 12). This coloration may be related to genetic, reproductive, or environmental factors. Young are more oval in shape. Their fins are tinted orange and finely edged with a blue-white border.

Not much in-depth field research has been performed regarding the five-cusped piranha. Its diet appears to be very similar to that of the genus *Pristobrycon,* being mainly vegetarian in nature. Masticated seeds are the dominant dietary component. Juveniles are known to consume large numbers of aquatic insects. Like the black-tailed piranha, this species occasionally finds its way into the tanks of importers, where young specimens are often not recognized as piranhas. Nothing is known about its reproductive biology. It would be interesting to learn if this most primitive of the piranhas practices the "advanced" behaviors of nest building and egg guarding. Perhaps some dedicated aquarist will someday provide us with the answers.

Genus *Catoprion*
Catoprion mento

Common name: Wimple piranha

Range: Another widespread species, being found throughout the Amazon Basin, the Orinoco and its tributaries, and the Paraná and Paraguay River systems

Adult size: Smaller than most true piranhas, adults average less than five inches (12.7 cm) in standard length

Comments: As I have discussed previously (pages 11 and 14), this species is not taxonomically a piranha. Its shape may be similar to that of many piranhas, but its unique dentition is adapted for removing scales from the bodies of living fishes. The wimple piranha is a solitary species, launching its attacks on other fishes from the cover of dense aquatic vegetation. It appears to prefer blackwater and clearwater habitats with little or no current. It is the only species so far known in its genus.

The markedly undershot lower jaw and attractive shape imparts a very unique appearance to this fish. In adults, the anterior rays of the dorsal

A freshly captured adult wimple piranha from the Rio Dimini drainage of northern Brazil.

and anal fins are prolonged into graceful streamers, and adult males develop a bilobed anal fin. A distinctive orange spot adorns the gill plate; this same color often suffuses the anal and ventral fins. The tail base is darkly pigmented. Young specimens lack the fin extensions, but otherwise closely resemble the adults. All studies have indicated that a large part of its diet consists of the scales of other fishes,

Juvenile wimple piranha. At this age the dorsal and anal fin extensions have not yet developed.

The author with a freshly caught adult red-bellied piranha. Aquarium specimens are rarely this colorful. Rio Orosa, Peru.

with smaller amounts of vegetable matter, fish fins, and aquatic insects also consumed.

Probably due to its attractive appearance, and small size at maturity, *Catoprion mento* is frequently imported. It also seems to lack the aggressiveness seen in most young true piranhas against members of its own species and can be safely kept in groups, at least when it is small. As can be imagined from its feeding habits, it is one of the world's worst community tank fish! I can find nothing about its breeding habits in the literature, and it has never been spawned in captivity. Here is another opportunity for the home aquarist to make a significant contribution to our ichthyological knowledge.

Useful Literature

Books

Géry, J. *Characoids of the World.* Neptune City, NJ: T.F.H. Publications, 1977.

Goulding, M. *The Fishes and the Forest: Explorations in Amazonian Natural History.* Los Angeles, CA: University of California Press, 1980.

Goulding, M, N. Smith and D. Mahar. *Floods of Fortune: Ecology and Economy Along the Amazon.* New York, NY: Columbia University Press, 1996.

Machado-Allison, A. *Los Peces de los Llanos de Venezuela: Un ensayo sobre su historia natural.* Caracas, Venezuela: Universida Central de Venezuela, 1987. (Spanish language)

Myers, G. (editor). *The Piranha Book: An Account of the Ill-Famed Piranha Fishes of the Rivers of Tropical South America.* Neptune City, NJ: T.F.H. Publications, 1972.

Roman, B. *Collección de los Peces de los Llanos de Venezuela,* III: Las Pirañas. Caracas, Venezuela: Fundacion Cientifica Fluvial de los Llanos, 1983. (Spanish language)

Schulte, W. *Piranhas in the Aquarium.* Neptune City, NJ: T.F.H. Publications, 1988.

Smith, N. J. H. *Man, Fishes, and the Amazon.* New York, NY: Columbia University Press, 1981.

References

In addition to the volumes listed, the reader is referred to the following papers as representative samples of the more current findings in piranha research.

Fink, W. and A. Machado-Allison. 1992. Three New Species of Piranhas from Brazil and Venezuela. *Ichthyological Explorations of Freshwaters,* 3(1):55–71.

Machado-Allison, A. 1985. Estudios sobre la sistemática de la subfamilia Serrasalminae. Part III: Sobre el estaus genérico y relaciones filogenéticus de los géneros *Pygopristis, Pygocentrus, Pristobrycon* y *Serrasalmus* (Teleostei-Characidae-Serrasalminae). *Acta Biologica Venezuelica,* 12(1):19–42 (summary in English; body of paper in Spanish).

Machado-Allison, A. and C. Garcia. 1986. Food Habits and Morphological Changes during Ontogeny in Three Serrasalmin Fish Species of the Venezuelan Floodplain, *Copeia,* 1986(1):193–196.

Nico, L. 1994. Nutritional Content of Piranha (Characide, Serrasalminae) Prey Items. *Copeia,* 1994(2),524–528.

———. 1991. Trophic Ecology of Piranhas (Characidae: Serrasalminae) from Savanna and Forest Regions in the Orinoco River Basin of Venezuela, 1991. University of Florida (Unpublished Doctoral Dissertation.)

Sazima, I. and F. A. Machado. 1990. Underwater Observations of Piranhas in Western Brazil. *Environmental Biology of Fishes,* 28:17–31.

Sazima, I, and S. de Andrade Guimaraes. 1987. Scavenging on Human Corpses as a Source for Stories about Man-eating Piranhas. *Environmental Biology of Fishes,* 20(1):75-77.

Uetanabaro, M., T. Wang, and S. A. Abe. 1993. Breeding Behavior of the Red-bellied Piranha, *Pygocentrus nattereri,* in Nature. *Environmental Biology of Fishes,* 36:369–371.

Winemiller, K. 1989. Odontogenic Diet Shifts and Resource Partitioning among Piscivorous Fishes in the Venezuelan llanos. *Environmental Biology of Fishes,* 26:177–179.

———. 1990. Caudal Eyespots as Deterrents against Fin Predation in the Neotropical Cichlid *Astronotus ocellatus. Copeia,* 1990(3):665–673.

Winemiller, K. and L. C. Kelso-Winemiller. 1993. Fin-nipping Piranhas. *National Geographic Research and Explorations,* 9(3):344–357.

Abbreviations, Tables of Equivalents, and Conversions

Abbreviations
Celsius or centigrade (°C)
centimeters (cm)
Fahrenheit (°F)
feet (ft)
grams (g)
gallons (gal)
inches (in)
kilograms (kg)
liters (L)
meters (m)
millimeters (mm)
milliliters (ml)
ounces (oz)
parts per million (ppm)

Equivalents
one centimeter equals
  100 millimeters
one foot equals 12 inches
one gallon equals 32 ounces
one gallon equals 4 quarts
one kilogram equals 1,000 grams
one meter equals
  1,000 millimeters
one milliliter equals
  (approximately) 25 drops
one tablespoon equals
  3 teaspoons

Temperature Conversions
Multiply Celsius by 1.8, then add 32 to obtain Fahrenheit. Subtract 32 from Fahrenheit reading, then multiply by 0.55 to obtain Celsius.

Conversions

Measurement	Multiplied by	Equals
centimeters	0.4	inches
inches	2.54	centimeters
feet	30.0	centimeters
grams	0.035	ounces
liters	1.06	quarts
millimeters	100.0	centimeters
millimeters	0.04	inches
pounds	0.45	kilograms
quarts	0.95	liters
teaspoons	5.0	milliliters

Index